# Man and the River:
## the Mississippi

# Hodding Carter

# Man and the River
## the Mississippi

Photography by Dan Guravich

**RAND McNALLY & COMPANY**

*Chicago • New York • San Francisco*

Jacket Illustration: Above La Crosse, Wisconsin

Book Design by Mili Thompson

*To the memory of Irma and Sarah*

# Contents

## Illustrations

# Man and the River:
## the Mississippi

# $\mathcal{T}$his river beside which I live...

# The River

This river beside which I live is made up, think some of us, of the spirit and muscle of God; and, at times, of Satan's own sinews.

For us who know and love and fear and profit from and delight in it, the Mississippi gives reason for great pride—not just that of the people of a rich and powerful mainstream and its valley, but the pride of man who has become the persistent tamer. For certainly in the history of mankind there is special place for such conflict between these protagonists, between man and the river, and for old tales and new of courage and brain and brawn, of the men who live beside and deal with the torrent that is in perpetual motion.

To understand the Mississippi River, the great divider and uniter of the North American continent, one must know that from the advent of the white man the 2,500-mile-long river has been recognized as not one but two great streams, an Upper and a Lower Mississippi, with the point of division coming at today's Cairo, Illinois, where the Ohio pours her drenching, accumulated volume into the river the Chippewas called the Mee-iss-see-bee, "father of waters."

But the Mississippi may be further divided into not two but four parts, for each of the two major divisions has one stretch where, by characteristics or use, it becomes distinctive.

The first of these begins where the Missouri brings its turbulence and dark red roiling into the Mississippi above St. Louis, marrying with the previously placid stream to endow it with the Missouri's own nature so that the Upper Mississippi which the Ohio meets is far different from the one the Missouri entered. This segment between the two major tributaries is sometimes called the Middle River.

The other separate identification may be given to the final 245 miles of the Lower Mississippi, where an inland waterway of great vitality becomes, from Baton Rouge south, a passageway which can accommodate to a draft of forty feet the seagoing vessels of the world. This is a seaman's river as well as a riverboatman's river, and dominating it is New Orleans, America's second port.

In the ten states which the Mississippi borders or traverses live more than 40 million people. Here are fishermen, farmers, industrialists, miners, boatmen, and followers of many another vocation common to American civilization or unique to the river valley.

Other and earlier societies than ours flourished on the banks of the Mississippi. The first

*Lock and Dam No. 3 near Harlis, Minnesota*

of which we have any record is that of the mound builders, who reared large earthen pyramids throughout a cultural corridor which ranged from Mexico to far up the Ohio. After the mound people came other Indians, coppery men with a different way of life. On this river they lived for a long time and the sons and daughters of these Indians are not yet dead. There is still the look of the Houmas and the Natchez and the Sioux and the Foxes in the faces of their descendants. Where they stood against the white man they lost. Where they did not stand against him they lost anyhow, from the lake country of the river's origins which bears as a state the Dakota Indian name of Minnesota, to the Louisiana marshes and the silt land at the Mississippi's delta.

Because of the white man's diseases and his yearning for the native women who bore light-skinned children for him (and thereby helped to destroy any unity or even pride of race), the birthright of the first Americans would have been lost had never an arrow been sent winging toward a white enemy, a Spanish lance dipped into dark flesh, or a rifle shot fired. But there was no way for the American Indian to stand up, save vainly, to the white soldier and explorer and trader. As had happened to hunters before, their forests would be felled and their hunting lands etched by the furrows of farms and by the interlacing of roads and streets.

Yet the white man did not find the conquest of the river land easy. The Mississippi challenged his possession of the fields he claimed, and the river itself was the foe—and mightier than any foeman the settlers faced on its banks, for the river could wipe out a man's lifetime of work in a day.

But they learned to live with the river even in its untamed days, and dared to build cities along its course—Minneapolis and St. Paul, Davenport and Rock Island, Moline and Muscatine, Alton and St. Louis and Memphis and Greenville, Vicksburg and Natchez and Baton Rouge and, nearer to its ending, New Orleans.

18

*New Orleans, Louisiana*

When the Canadian brothers Lemoyne, the Sieurs d'Iberville and de Bienville, entered the river from the south on Mardi Gras Day in 1699, they could not have foreseen what would be wrought here. Nor could Bienville have seen this far into the future when he founded in 1718, in a sickly place, the first town on the Lower Mississippi, New Orleans, intended as a defense against Indians and encroaching Englishmen and with the objective of domination of trade. Nor could the French and Canadian woodsmen and soldiers, who were vassals to a homeland that was all but unknown to them.

In 1832 another white man would determine for himself and for almost everyone else the source of the river that was so far north in Minnesota. His name was Henry Schoolcraft and he was at home among the Ojibways and

*Lake Itasca, Minnesota*

Sioux to whom the government had dispatched him, an Indian agent, to pacify the quarreling tribes. Possessed of a classical mind, he gave to what he designated as the river's source a name he created from parts of two Latin words, *veritas* and *caput*—"true head"—so that it remains today as Lake Itasca.

And if this concourse is inseparable now from the fortunes of the people of America, what of its importance for the future? Water is more precious to man than any sustaining element save for the breath of life itself, and water is as requisite to man as that very air. How fortunate a people who have such a river as the Mississippi! Man has not yet found nor wishes to find a way to dry it up, but through his carelessness he could convert too easily a vital, multipurpose river into an open sewage canal.

Long before the Mississippi River ever was, its future course was being set by powers infinitely greater even than its own, powers still in operation. For 200,000 centuries, wash from the Appalachians and from the Ozarks and Ouachitas had been cast east and west in an ever-deepening wedge on the floor of an ancient gulf, until finally the sheer weight of the Mesozoic and Cenozoic sediments downwarped the very bedrock. Into the trough thus created tumbled the accumulated mass which deepened in spots to 20,000 feet and in which oil pools formed, later covered by alluvial deposits.

North of this gulf other earth movements depressed the Central Gulf Plain north and south, breaking through the Gulf coast geosyncline, permitting the ocean to pour into the Mississippi structural trough, and forming thereby a great inland sea, the Mississippi embayment, as wide as 200 miles and ranging northward 600 miles to today's Commerce, Missouri.

Stresses which still exist within the earth's crust caused other faults, faults that depressed the areas in the bottom of the embayment and correspondingly upended other parts to produce the sediment-covered hills of southern Mississippi. These hills turn the present river westward for a distance and narrow the alluvial valley, just as uplifts near today's Monroe, Louisiana, and below, in south central Louisiana, force it east.

Deep beneath the Ice Age debris and silt which drown them, steep valleys formed by later earth faultings control the southeastward direction of the St. Francis, the White-Arkansas, the Ouachita, and the Red, and the Yazoo's tributary

21

Tallahatchie and its tributary the Coldwater southwestward. These built their own deltas in the alluvial plain which was gradually being formed, first by the sediment carried by unknown, unnamed rivers, and later by the Mississippi.

So long as men were few in the valley and they could readily move their encampments to dry ridges, they bowed to nature's will and moved as the river's rises and falls required. But with the coming of settlers who demanded permanent abodes, the effort to master the river began.

For the first Europeans who cleared the cane and felled the oak and cypress along the riverside, there was room aplenty on the sites they selected, the hills and bluffs or the high banks of the river itself or the ridges marking a long-ago meander. For this must be remembered, that the Lower Mississippi is an alluvial stream and as

*At Scott, Mississippi*

such builds its own insufficient confinement. At flood, without the control man has learned to impose, it crosses its banks and, slowing as it spreads, drops its loam. In time, the heightening embankment rises above any but the highest flood. From behind this barrier the water has no way to return directly to the river but must journey back tortuously, by old paths, and through the openings made by the tributary streams. Sometimes these themselves, in flood at the same time as the river, back up to a section of the riverbank and make of it a narrow island.

But even the natural riverfront could not assure safety, as the Frenchmen at New Orleans learned in their first few years. The ditches the government required them to dig around each house site, as a requirement of ownership, were expected to sluice the swirling overflow toward the cypress swamp behind the town, but this was no protection in a higher than expected spring rise. In 1731 Governor Etienne de Périer ordered earthen embankments thrown up high enough to keep the water out of the city—*levées* the Frenchmen called them, meaning "lifted up."

And so the pattern was set. Wherever man in the lower valley would raise his home, a levee would follow, low for those generations in which the crest could spread from hills to hills but, as levee joined levee and more land was cleared, taller and broader they grew to hold back the growing volume of water contained between artificial banks. In time, all but continuous levees would be erected from riverside high point to riverside bluff along the whole Mississippi from above Davenport, Iowa, to below New Orleans.

Levees alone would prove insufficient instruments for control of the river, and man would devise supplements for impressing his will on the force which he must master or be mastered by. And simultaneously with this taming, man put his autocratic hand upon the wild river's vagaries, so that the waterway once traveled by canoe, or portaged where rapids and lengthy bends required, would be shaped to the needs of this day.

25

# $\mathcal{T}$he Wildlife

Go back in time now to the days when no man built the ceremonial and burying mounds and no Houmas lashed flint point to slim, straight shaft and no white man had usurped river and forest and the darker man's villages. Go back to the days when wild things roamed unchallenged; when the river was where the buffalo trail ended, and the wolves crunched upon animals less strong, and the shadows of the passenger pigeons who fly no more were a canopy that spread from wilderness bank to sandbar and uncharted channel and floating islands of drift. Other wilderness breeds are departed, too, but the savory buck still leaps affrighted at the call of the hunter's horn and the baying of the hound and the hoof-thud of the huntsman's horse.

And it must not be forgotten that in the swamps and forests along the Mississippi, the hunted creatures will know you are there and be wary of your presence just as the human poachers resent the patrolling game wardens, and the degraded human beings whom we call river rats fiercely resent the oil barges and the towboats that rock their boats as they fish.

The buffalo that once grazed in the Mississippi Valley from the north to almost the south end has galloped now into the lost past, because man never stops slaying wildlife; and no riverman knows, as his forebears knew, the pathways the buffalo took to water and grazing land. Few black bears shuffle through the river's underbrush and forest, rising on their hind legs now and then to look about for enemies or food.

There have been times when more fur was trapped among the giant reeds of the marshlands and bayou country below New Orleans than in all of Canada and Alaska put together. Muskrat and beaver and mink from the Mississippi country still supply much of the world's needs, just as its furs did when the Canadian trappers and the Indians transported their pelts to the trading posts by canoe. The imported nutria which domesticated in Louisiana almost too easily has learned to live with its neighbor, the muskrat, though for a while the strong-toothed scrapper threatened to eradicate the native creature.

And the Mississippi Valley, for its entire length, is the greatest American flyway. Singing or chattering with the advancing season, mockingbirds and redwing blackbirds, robins and crested flycatchers and yellow-bellied sapsuckers, ruby-throated hummingbirds and purple martins move to new shelters from the tupelo and maple and ash and cypress and live oaks and wild pecan trees and brush and clearings behind the low

26

*North of Benoit, Mississippi*

levees near the delta, to find summer homes as far north as Lake Itasca or beyond. Near the willow-fringed shores and in still pools and sloughs left by a falling river, and on sandbars and islands, migratory waterfowl find rest in the series of wildlife refuges from Minnesota to the Gulf provided by the Fish and Wildlife Service of the U.S. Department of the Interior.

Down the Mississippi flyway in the fall, and northward in the spring, streak with military precision the ducks and the Canadian and blue geese and lesser gaggles and flights, and they are more protected now than ever before in history. Some people don't like this protection, which sets strict limits on duck and goose and turkey. These people we call game hogs. And there are too many of them.

The Mississippi flyway and the riverside lands were not made for hunters and hunted alone. A French naturalist of mysterious antecedents who was known as John James Audubon could have told us this more than 140 years ago as he went about his dedicated task of preserving with paint and brush the image of wild turkey, the heron, the multiplicity of birds—even the buzzard —and some beasts of the lower valley. With miles upon miles of shores kept in their natural state today as wildlife refuges, the river's virgin banks and sandbars and chutes and coulees provide a rare ecological, recreational landscape. For nowhere else on the North American continent can wildlife, in the forests and beneath the waters of the river and its smaller feeders and even in the violated havens, be found in such a variety of animals and birds and fish as along the Mississippi's course.

If there is anything lovelier than wild creatures in their natural state and unaware of or indifferent to the presence of man, I don't know what it could be. I have hunted the deer and the wild boar and the small, deceptive doves. And time and again I have marveled that I could destroy freedom and beauty in a world so in need of both. In earlier years, before I got around to discovering this truth for myself, I did my full

29

share of killing. I have hunted duck in bayous and inlets and from hidden blinds, and shot dove from the gleaned fields of corn and soybeans. I have shot grouse and pheasant and quail near the upper reaches of the Mississippi, and mean, long-tusked boar little more than ten miles from our town of Greenville, Mississippi. I have shot coon out of treetops and they make good eating, baked with a thick, pungent gravy, especially if there is no other meat in a deer-luckless camp.

I have never killed an alligator, though I have tried, but I have killed poisonous water moccasins and a few rattlesnakes. From the banks of the river I have netted the tiny, succulent river shrimp, the best shrimp of them all. And I have fished for crappie and bream in the water below a river dam or along the shores of an oxbow lake and cast for bigmouth bass along a willow-bordered, river-fed lake whose tree waterline betrays the height of the spring rising. And once on a jug fishing expedition I gigged a catfish that measured almost five feet in length. In jug fishing —to explain to the uninitiated—empty, gaudily painted gallon jugs float downstream, each dangling a heavy cord and hook and smelly bait from its corked mouth. The fisherman's boat

follows lazily. When the catfish strikes, under go jug and fish and both remain there until the fish's strength is gone. Then both erupt into the air and the fisherman approaches to pull in his catch. Incidentally, you don't scale a catfish. You nail him against a tree or a barn and—since he has no scales, but a heavy, tough skin—you skin him.

When I think of the river and the creatures who live beside it, it is the deer which is uppermost in my mind. Man has hunted the deer on every continent and with spear and arrow and rifle and shotgun pellets. In the north woods the

hunter stalks the deer. In our part of the valley the old ways of England persist. The hunters scatter throughout the designated forests and await the coming of the driven deer. These are pursued by men on horseback, blowing blasts upon their hunting horns behind packs of deerhounds that could be the descendants of the long, lithe hunting dogs that yelped through the glades of England in the hunting of the hart.

There is beauty in the hunt. Once a majestic buck burst through the woods close by my own stand. He paused for a moment and looked about and saw me and bounded away with a magnificent

*Catfish Point, Mississippi*

swiftness. I might have shot at him, but I couldn't. In seconds the pack followed, not bunched together but scattered so that I saw only two or three; and behind the dogs, the horses, undeterred by the thickets and brambles that tore at them.

When one of my sons brought down his first mallards, one of the ducks hit me on the shoulder as it fell where I was waist-deep in the bayou, picking up a couple that I had knocked down a little while earlier. I was so proud of his marksmanship that I didn't fuss at him until sometime later for shooting over a man's head, especially his father's.

But I have done more among the wild things of the river than kill them. I have watched while the white herons came undulating like an odalisque's fan, by the hundreds and even the thousands, through the cypress and willow. I have seen the pelican in flight, and he is a different bird from the ungainly waddler with the top-heavy beak, so laughable on the ground and so beautifully sober as he sits perched on a jetty's piling in the muddy, treeless delta. I have seen does with their fawns who sometimes come so close that they can lick your face, as one young buck once licked mine when I was napping behind a log. And I have seen the wild turkey gobbler strut and soar unharmed because my fellow huntsmen and I had reached our limit. I have seen a braver man than I thrust his arm into a hollow log and drag out the spitting, clawing wildcat and laugh at the lacework of lacerations on his hand.

The Mississippi was home to the wild things before settlers ever staked their claims or nations ever declared their boundaries. It still is.

Some say that advancing civilization and overhunting will destroy the river's game. I don't believe it. There is enough untillable and heavily forested land left on the river to form a natural preserve for uncounted generations to come. My worry is not that the deer and the turkey and the boar and the mallard will disappear. Rather it is that man with his talent for self-destruction may disappear along with his prey.

# The People

What of man and his ways on the river? This we do know, that when recorded time began in the valley in the sixteenth century, men who could write described a coppery people who dwelt by the riverside and in the shadow of great mounds built by men who had gone before.

No primitive American people loom larger or more mysteriously than the mound builders who were Indians, many different Indians who for many different reasons and over the course of fifteen centuries chose to erect earthworks of different types and sizes. Three thousand years ago these men of another culture were rearing their mounds in the Ohio and Mississippi valleys for uses not clearly understood today. The eroded remains of these oldest of mounds haunt the imagination. So do the smaller conical mounds for the burial of the dead which began to be built at the time of Christ. These, like the linear earthworks which outline the shapes of turtles, birds, and snakes and which were contemporary with them, also stand today along the entire riverside.

Almost a thousand years later, from A.D. 900 to 1200, came another building period, and what is called the Mississippi Culture spread eastward and southward from its seed place in the Upper Mississippi. Atop the very high cere-monial mounds of this period, perpetual fires burned in the wooden lodges and on the altars at today's Cahokia in Illinois, where stand the greatest mounds of all, and at Winterville in Mississippi, where fifteen of the twenty-three mounds first noted there by white men can still be counted, and at hundreds of other sites throughout the valley. And while the Mississippi Culture evolved, the use of the snake symbol spread like an epidemic across the North American continent from Oklahoma to the eastern seaboard and up and down the great rivers of the interior. The huge earthen snakes—designed, like the mounds, as potent religious manifestations—became relics of a cult which rapidly burned itself out.

The earthen snakes, like the mounds, were constructed by the women. Patiently, clay and dirt were packed into handwoven baskets, poured onto soil already carried to the site, trampled and impacted by bare or moccasined feet, and covered by another basketful as tediously assembled, until in time a mound had risen to eighty feet, to ninety, to a hundred, and thousands of cubic yards of dirt had been moved. Hundreds upon hundreds of mounds of all sizes were erected, so that almost every town along the river has or has had its example, for the men who came later

would wisely choose the same high terrain that the first comers had made their own.

The mound builders of the Mississippi Valley and of the Ohio and of southeastern Texas became a vanished people shortly after the white man discovered the evidence of their being. We do not know whence they came, whither they went, or what they did in the centuries between their coming and their leave-taking. But what of this disappearance?—this vanishing of a whole people who represent but a fraction of a moment in infinity yet leave us with a numbing wonder, for man does not consider himself as a calculable or incalculable fraction of anything.

We know only that the mound builders were not a sedentary people living in permanent abodes, nor were they altogether nomads or lacking in a religious and political culture. The mounds they built are proof enough; heavy, truncated, and sometimes conical, they served more than one purpose. They were religious meccas. They were burial grounds for the chieftains. They were the centers of government, and they must have been, to the people who camped in their shadows when the season was ended, proof of unity and a people's will to survive.

Modern man has not treated the mounds well nor has nature. The mounds have eroded; some of them have been bulldozed to the level of the surrounding farmland; they have been carelessly dug into and scarred and put to use as slit silos and sites for homes. But, nevertheless, they tell us that a people, probably Indian, whom we call mound builders once found the Mississippi to their liking and lived beside it three times as many years as has the white man. And they and their civilization are gone.

History begins in the Mississippi Valley with the arrival of the white man, who brought not only his gun to destroy what he found, but his pen to describe it. Individual triumphs and failures would be recorded along with those of nations as they strove for possession of the land and for the allegiance of the river's people.

Hernando de Soto and his fellow explorer-killers were the first Europeans to see the river. They reached it on May 8, 1541, somewhere between Tunica County, the most northern area of northwest Mississippi, and the Chickasaw Bluffs, below Memphis. The first report ever written about the Mississippi described it in flood. Its author is known to us only as the Gentleman of Elvas:

"It was nearly a half league wide, and if a man stood still on the other side one could not tell whether he were a man or something else. It was of great depth, and of very strong current. Its waters were always turgid and continually many trees and wood came down it, borne along by the force of the current. . . . It had abundance of fish of various kinds and most of them different from those of the fresh waters of Spain."

For a year before this the expedition had remained on the east side of the river, pillaging, killing, looking for treasure, before its members built small boats and crossed to the other side. A year later de Soto died. His soldiers buried him secretly in the river and a lieutenant, Luis de Moscosco, took command. The dwindling party of Spaniards built crude boats, and Moscosco and the other survivors fought their way downstream against Indians lining both banks, who showered them with arrows and sought to capsize their canoes. Incredibly, some reached the mouth of the river and sailed across the Gulf to Panuco, Mexico, where Spain had control of the coast.

How well or how bitterly the Indians remembered the Spaniards, who like their horses came roughshod to the river, is not known. But for more than a century and a quarter they might have congratulated themselves that they were spared a new revelation of this higher civilization. Meanwhile, for many of the Indians a strange death had come, not from the actual presence of the white man but from his diseases that traveled ahead of him from wherever he landed on the coasts. Between the coming of de Soto and the appearance of the next white men on the Mississippi, thousands on thousands of Indians would

*Port Gibson, Mississippi*

die. In one geographical area, the broad delta of the Yazoo-Mississippi conjunction, they would be entirely wiped out.

And quiet rolled the river, without written record of its racing currents or its summer-shrunk channels. Silently, then as now, whole oak trees standing as though on islands floated by on mattings of debris torn from caving banks in springtime flood or late fall rise. On prairies and bluffs, on hills and in the floodplain, tribesmen of a culture different from that of the mound builders fished or stalked game which the squaws cooked along with the maize they had ripped from the stick-scratched earth. In the north the Sioux and Foxes and Chippewas and Dakotas and Illinois, farther south the Choctaws and Chickasaws, the Natchez and the Bayogoulas, the Quinipissas and Mongoulachas and Houmas and Taensas took what they needed from forest and stream, fought as men do for infringements on right or for unfair advantage.

To the river each tribe had given a name, among them the Chippewas. That name would persist for the Canadians and Frenchmen, whose imagination burned with the sound, and who next sought the great river, inscribed the word for a world to know: Mee-iss-see-bee.

These next white newcomers to the river were not murderous adventurers, torturing and slaying in the search for gold, but traders seeking furs. And side by side with them in the canoes rode missionaries seeking souls. The French would deal with the Indians in an easy camaraderie which would build strong alliances against an encroaching seaboard people of still another ancestry, who wanted to settle and fell the forests and till the land rather than range the woods and acquire peltries by chase and trap and trade.

But that competition was still in the future when, in the spring of 1673, the first Frenchmen reached the Mississippi. Their descriptions stoked the fire of westward exploration.

Characteristically, the two French trailblazers were a trader and a priest; and the trader, Louis Jolliet, was actually one of a still newer breed, a native and white North American. Born at Beaupré, near Quebec, he had been sent to France for a year of scientific studies. Father Jacques Marquette, the Jesuit priest, born in Laon, France, had prayed that he might go to the wilds and become a missionary and die in the wilderness when his time should come. His gentleness was almost that of a saint.

Louis Jolliet, of all men of his time, best knew the country of the Great Lakes, the most westerly of French-Canadian lands. Father Marquette had perfected himself in knowledge of the Illinois tongue, and listening to the Illinois tribesmen, he was able to understand what they told of a great river which they had crossed. Unwittingly each man had prepared himself for his historic role.

To Marquette's Huron mission of St. Ignace on the north shore of the Straits of Mackinac came Jolliet in December 1672, with the welcome news that he had been commissioned by Governor Frontenac to seek the legendary stream of which the missionary had told him, and that the priest was to accompany him as chaplain. After a winter of planning, Father Marquette and Louis Jolliet left St. Ignace in two bark canoes with five voyageurs as paddlers. Across the long Lake Michigan, down to the head of what now is Green Bay, and up the Fox they went to the Mascouten village, near today's Berlin, Wisconsin, the outer limits of water trails known to the French. From that village, Indians guided them across the mile-long swampy portage to the Wisconsin. And on June 17, 1673, a month after leaving St. Ignace, the two canoes shot out into the Mississippi, having followed a way used immemorially by the Indians and now a sensational discovery of the white men.

With the current, they traveled downriver for a month more. At the mouth of the Arkansas they learned from tribesmen of the presence of other white men farther south. Having ascertained the Mississippi emptied into the Gulf, they decided that they would leave Indians and any chance Spaniards from Mexico to themselves and return to Canada with the tidings that would give Europe knowledge of new lands to conquer.

Up the river and thence into the Illinois they raced to the Des Plaines. Canoeing through the future site of Chicago, they entered Lake Michigan, bearing their charts and records with them. Their reports opened a new period of questing. And had not wars kept the attention of England and France fixed on European battlegrounds, rather than on the New World's fields of conquest, the Mississippi would the sooner have seen colonies of white men on its far distant shores.

Following Marquette and Jolliet to the river was the Sieur de La Salle, who first proposed a colony on the Mississippi's banks. A Frenchman, a dreamer who could organize nothing, a stiff-necked man who irritated many of his followers but had devoted, self-sacrificing close friends, a venturer who sleeps in an unmarked grave in Texas—La Salle has as his monument the opening of the Mississippi Valley for colonization, though he planted no colony upon its banks. He was, however, the first Frenchman to see its mouth and the first to send explorers to visit its upper reaches. And he envisioned an empire for France stretching from eastern Canada to the Gulf. Most importantly, because of him France claimed the Mississippi Valley as her own.

La Salle had come to Canada in 1666 to recoup the fortune surrendered when he took preliminary vows as a Jesuit. From his seigneury, derisively nicknamed La Chine, this visionary would not go forth to discover a new route to China; instead, through him France achieved title to a new and vast empire.

Restless because he was tied down by the responsibilities of estate management, La Salle returned the seigneury to the Sulpicians who had made it available to him, and for eight years he roamed the forests north of the Ohio. Thus when word came that Jolliet and Marquette had passed the mouth of the Ohio and gone even farther south, on the Mississippi, La Salle realized that someone would profit from their discoveries and that he and his sponsor, Governor Frontenac,

must act at once to get the fur trading rights in Ohio territory, which was now delineated and much of which he had traversed. Fur rights were exclusive privileges entitling the holder to a monopoly to trade with the Indians for furs, which were natural resources more immediately wealth-producing than the oil for which later explorers of undeveloped countries would seek the concessions.

Going to France in 1674, the tall nobleman returned with the king's favor, and three years later he was accorded the monopoly over an even wider area for the trade in buffalo and lesser furs. More importantly, on his second trip to France, in 1677, La Salle acquired the services of Henri de Tonty, twenty-eight-year-old French-born son of an Italian father. In time this valued lieutenant would know the river's tribes and trails as would no other white man, and Tonty's name, in justice, should grace at least as many buildings from the Illinois to the Gulf as does La Salle's.

La Salle established a shipyard on the St. Lawrence above the wondrous Niagara Falls and there, with Tonty in charge, built the *Griffon*, the better to fetch buffalo peltries from the West. Sailing it to Green Bay, La Salle loaded the *Griffon* richly and sent it eastward while he and Tonty and his chaplain, the Récollet friar, Father Zenobius Membré, canoed up the St. Joseph and down the Kankakee and the Illinois. On this river in February 1680, he built Fort Crève Coeur and from here in the spring he dispatched three men to make the first exploration of the Upper Mississippi and to bring back furs.

But La Salle seemed fated to fail. The *Griffon* sailed to oblivion; his creditors demanded immediate settlement, which forced La Salle to return east to appease them; Tonty, in charge of Fort Crève Coeur, was deserted by his men and had to abandon the fort; the three men sent to the Upper Mississippi were captured by the Sioux. These three—Michel Aco, Antoine Auguel, and Father Louis Hennepin, a large-framed Récollet whose colorful report became an inter-

*Dubuque, Iowa*

*Quincy, Illinois*

national best seller—were subjected to many indignities and would have been put to death except for the providential arrival of Daniel Greysolon, Sieur du L'hut. Earlier, du L'hut (often called Duluth) had intrepidly performed the dangerous and all but impossible feat of bringing the Sioux and their traditional enemy, the Chippewas, into concord—so that their strife would not stop the white man's westward expansion. Escorted in friendship and in triumph by the Sioux to their great encampment at Mille Lacs, he had there taken possession of their country in the name of Louis XIV. Their hunting grounds included the headwaters of the Mississippi, though such streams as du L'hut had seen he could not have known to be early tributaries of the river. Du L'hut had returned to Lake Superior after this great coup. Then, coming back down the St. Croix into the Mississippi, he heard of the capture of the three Frenchmen. Thanks to his popularity with the Indians, he succeeded in scolding them into liberating La Salle's representatives. He himself guided the freed prisoners back to Mackinac. That La Salle's agents had indeed visited the Upper Mississippi is attested by Father Hennepin's record that he had seen certain falls and had given them the name they still bear, the Falls of St. Anthony.

La Salle, meanwhile, rejoined by Tonty, built a new fort on the upper Illinois near today's Ottawa and from this Fort St. Louis, in early 1682, he, Tonty, Father Membré, twenty other Frenchmen and thirty-one Indians, including women and children, set out to explore the lower course of the great river. On February 6 they passed from the Illinois into the Mississippi and arrived at its mouth two months later. Here, on April 9, La Salle took possession of the river and all the lands it drained, naming the territory in the Sun King's honor—Louisiana, for Louis XIV. Father Membré signed the act of possession.

Now indeed had come the time to confirm possession of the inland empire by planting a colony near the Mississippi, which La Salle called the River Colbert, complimenting Louis XIV's colonial minister.

War between Spain and France postponed the king's acceptance of La Salle's initial proposal, and two years later when the explorer opened his sealed orders, he found that he had been directed to establish a colony, not so much for the longtime development of the river as for a point of departure from which raids against Spain's Mexican gold mines might be made! La Salle had implied to the king that Tonty would bring 4,000 Indian warriors down from Fort St. Louis to aid in such a filibuster, the first of the many to be plotted with the Mississippi River area as its base.

Thus when La Salle failed to turn his ships into the mouth of the river, his orders as well as golden visions made him ignore the fresh water which so obviously meant a river's delta. Onward and westward across the Gulf he sailed to the Texas coast where he established a base.

For two years Tonty ranged up and down the valley searching for his commander, whom he had expected to meet on the Mississippi. Along the way he left his brightly hued coat with the friendly Bayogoulas as a sign for La Salle that he had been there, that he had lived up to his obligation and loyalty. He later learned that La Salle had been murdered by one of his men and the colony on the Gulf coast had been wiped out.

If La Salle had dreamed of an empire—and he had—Tonty, making friends and allies for France from the mouth of the Illinois to the mouth of the Mississippi, knew of what the wealth might soonest consist. He wrote in his *Mémoire:*

"As for the Mississippi, it could produce every year 20,000 *écus*' worth of peltries, an abundance of lead, and wood for ship-building. A silk trade might be established there, and a port for the protection of vessels and the maintenance of a community with the Gulf of Mexico. Pearls might be found there. If wheat will not grow at the lower part of the river, the upper country could furnish it: and the islands might be supplied with everything they need, such as planks, vegetables, grain and salt beef . . . ."

Who was the greater visionary? I think Tonty, the brave Frenchman. In time, from the valley would move timber and minerals and foodstuffs and manufactured products, not only enough for the isles of the Caribbean, as Tonty had prophesied, but for Latin America and for Europe and the rest of the world.

But whose hands would bring fruition to the valley? Whose methods and systems would prevail?

In England Dr. Daniel Coxe, whose patent gave him title to the province of Carolina stretching from sea to sea between the thirty-first and thirty-sixth parallels, provisioned ships and Huguenot settlers for a colony on the Mississippi. To block such thrustings, which would link an English river to an English coast, and to protect France's claim to the waterway, which from the South, like the St. Lawrence from the East, provided a natural highway to the heart of the continent, Louis XIV mounted an expedition of his own. He placed in charge a Canadian who knew the New World, the naval hero Pierre Lemoyne, Sieur d'Iberville, who had distinguished himself with success on Hudson Bay against the omnipresent enemy, the English.

Leaving the *Badine* and the *Marin*, which had convoyed his party from France, at a Gulf coast anchorage he had named Ship Island, Iberville sailed westward with a party of some fifty men in two *traversiers*, each towing a bark canoe, in search of the river La Salle had claimed. Fresh water they saw, but the river mouth was blocked by what they believed to be huge palisades of rock, some as high as six feet and some as large as an acre. Closer, they discovered that the rocks were in fact large mud lumps. In 1686 the Spaniard Barroto, cruising the Gulf, had sighted such a delta and called the hidden river the River of the Palisades. These lumps at the mouth of the Mississippi are identifying characteristics, forced up by subterranean pressure and

unique to this delta.

Coming through the North Pass, the Frenchmen made their way to the first solid land beyond the reedy marshes above the Head of the Passes and there, on that night of March 3, 1699, camped at the spot they called Mardi Gras, because it was indeed the day before Lent. Thus the name of the first site on the Lower River tied land and the Christian year into a yet indestructible unity.

Iberville continued upstream intent upon imposing France's domination on a land whose dark people knew no such concept. All but unnoted was a six-mile-wide intervention of land between the river and a large lake on the right. Iberville's young brother Bienville stored the knowledge in his mind and nineteen years later founded here the city of New Orleans, a place from which could be controlled the commerce of a fertile and not fully developed valley.

Iberville was anxious to ascertain if this river he had entered from the Gulf was indeed the one La Salle had claimed. The fact was established hearteningly and brilliantly when the Bayogoulas showed him the coat Tonty had left as a sign for La Salle.

With proof sufficient to substantiate France's claim against all comers, Iberville directed the rest of the party to return to the Mississippi Sound the way the boats had come. Meanwhile he, with four Frenchmen and an Indian guide, explored what some Indians had described as a fork in the river. This passage toward the Gulf began by bayou, the lower valley's name for a channel letting out the river's surplus which, before levees, streamed across the natural bank in spring's high water. The Ascantia, as the Indians called this particular bayou, spun eastward off the Mississippi and then connected with a river which today is called Amite. From there a waterway through Lakes Maurepas and Pontchartrain and Borgne led into the sound, which is embraced by the islands of the Gulf.

The way was slow. In the Ascantia, which would later be called Bayou Manchac and

Iberville River, Iberville made ten portages in a scant seven miles. Yet it was an outlet for the Mississippi to the Gulf and it would have its impressive days in history, for the frequently nonexistent stream bounded what the treaty makers of four countries would call the Isle of Orleans, that land which was bordered by the Iberville, the lakes, the Gulf of Mexico, and the Mississippi River.

A momentous six months after Iberville's entry in 1699 into the river, the English corvette *Carolina Galley*, bearing Coxe's Huguenots, sailed up the Mississippi to within sight of where now stands the city of New Orleans and learned that the race for the river was already won. Bienville, coming downstream, discovered the ship anchored and awaiting favorable winds. He told its Captain Bond, whom he recognized, that the French were around the bend in force. Bienville had been with his brother Iberville at the Hudson's Bay engagement in which the captain had once before known defeat at the hands of the French. Believing Bienville's bluff, Captain Bond, the *Carolina Galley*, and the settlers for England withdrew. Thus was it set that the first white men to profit from the river would be French.

But Bienville, who succeeded his brother as governor of Louisiana, had to spend much of his time combating the machinations of English traders, who came down the Ohio and the Mississippi as far as the Arkansas and among the Chickasaws. To maintain France's hold, the Louisiana colony needed a settlement on the Mississippi.

In France, John Law, a Scotsman who was manipulating Louis XV's bankrupt treasury, envisioned the colony as the foundation in a pyramid of prosperity, which he portrayed in glowing terms that captivated the imagination of French and German investors and resulted in the first North American land boom. Maps of the "rapidly developing colony" were distributed in 1717, and Law's Company of the Indies, as is the wont of promoters, showed the city of New Orleans on the map, although as yet there was no such town.

Some months later, Bienville, on orders from France, did start clearing the designated site, using the labor of convicts who had been expatriated for bootlegging salt in violation of the Crown monopoly. Along a nearby bayou leading from Lake Pontchartrain, a few Canadians had built their primitive homes. To those already on the Isle of Orleans were now added unwilling settlers: Frenchmen, driven from the prisons of their homeland, and sturdy Germans, seduced by Law's hyperbolic descriptions into coming to a country which was far different from what the prospectuses had described. Too poor to go home, they had to remain.

John Law's Mississippi Bubble burst, and the colonists he had sent or lured to the snake-infested, mosquito-darkened land of wretched climate were abandoned on their ill-drained arpents and small town lots to make for themselves whatever future they could.

France looked to this sickly colony for indigo and deerskins and lumber and to the ill-provisioned garrison of reluctant soldiers and the diplomacy of the fur trade for control of Louisiana, sprawling northward to the Illinois River. Two fur posts, Kaskaskia and Cahokia, south of that river, were established in 1720 and protected by Fort Chartres, which was erected between them as one in a chain of fortifications that ran from Canada to the Gulf. But the colony was supported only in desultory fashion by the Bourbons, who were otherwise engaged at home, and by the Canadian French, who feared Louisiana would draw off the furs previously shipped through the St. Lawrence River towns.

The trading posts and bateaux were crammed with axes and bright cloth and knives and beads and mirrors and baubles, articles of European clothing and small luxuries and, eventually, muskets and powder and brandy and wine, for the Indian in America has ever been too great a temptation to the civilized white man ready to turn a quick penny, honestly or not.

It was for the French trade goods and the English trade goods that the Indians of the valley virtually gave away a fortune in pelts. Downriver sped the long, broad Indian freight canoes laden with the skins of deer and buffalo and beaver, bear and mink and muskrat and any wild animal whose fur could be found useful by the hatters and clothiers and shoemakers and robe fashioners of Europe. But no one was ever really satisfied: not the Indians, because they thought they were being paid unfairly low prices for their furs; not the French trappers and trading post officers, because they thought they were being underpaid, too; and not the government, because, furs or no,

the Louisiana colony was not turning into the cornucopia from which would spill the wealth of the New World. But the Indian and the white man continued to trade in peltries long after these had ceased to be the most desirable of Mississippi Valley commodities and, though not over as broad an expanse as formerly, the fur trade continues today. St. Louis, which was founded as a fur post, is still fur center for the mid-continent.

Had the Indians been united in a massive confederation, the white man would not have lasted a year, except by sufferance. But the Indians were not united. Instead, they were in

many separate tribes, large and small, with few confederations. They warred intermittently and few smoked the pipe of peace with each other. The white man's triumph over them in the Mississippi Valley came because he rarely had to face a united foe. Instead he could almost always count on Indians to join in killing the enemy which they so wrongly believed to be more dangerous than the English—or the French.

Only once in the early years of the white man's tenuous hold did the Indians rise against the encroaching power. Spearheaded by the Natchez, a tribe derived from the high culture of the mound builders and governed by theocratic

rulers, they attacked Fort Rosalie at today's Natchez. The Indians slaughtered 250 colonists and captured 230 women and children and more than 200 slaves. It was a major stroke against the white man's establishment.

Inexorably, the exponents of the new culture that had come to the river pursued the Natchez, defeated them, and forced the few survivors to flee eastward to the protection of England's Chickasaw allies.

But the Indians had made clear their message: There were limits beyond which they could not be pushed. However, others were to be enslaved.

From the founding of the Louisiana colony and in growing numbers after the Natchez revolt, African natives—defeated in tribal wars and sold to slave traders by the victors—were brought in chains to river and bayou, some having become conditioned to their lot on the French islands of the Caribbean. Thousands of miles from home, separated from the people of their own tribe, working next to men whose tongues they did not know, they were stood over by slave drivers and promptly punished for any resistance. The public rack awaited their chiefs, and even their women who joined in conspiracies were tracked by dogs through the unknown and terror-infested cypress swamps. The history of the slave revolts would be suppressed on the theory that what is not talked of may go away. Somehow, revolt by slaves seemed different from revolution by free men.

Yet the hard arms and gleaming backs of these Africans, who had been brought to the colony in large shipments, cleared the Lower River lands. Their sweat watered the blood-red flower of future civil war and strife.

During the century and more of Europe's domination of the Mississippi, the river's mouth lay three months distant from the nations which grasped for its control. But ownership of Silesia brought on the Seven Years' War, which imposed new allegiances on the river dwellers; resulted in death as political martyrs for five merchants and planters of New Orleans; caused Pontiac, chief of the Ottawas, to lead a campaign against England; and required a slight change of plans for certain French traders who held the Osage Indian fur monopoly.

As the Seven Years' War neared its end in 1762, Louis XV, painfully cognizant of who would be the victor, gave to his Bourbon cousin, Charles III of Spain, the Isle of Orleans and all his Louisiana colony west of the Mississippi, so that at least this much would not fall into the hands of England, the enemy. Louis figured rightly. At the end of the war France would lose all her North American holdings and for the first time the Mississippi River would serve, for much of its length, as an international boundary, with Spain on one side and England on the other. The river valley would be cut in two.

While rumors of the transfer reached Louisiana in 1763, Spain, which had reluctantly accepted the expense of running the colony, kept deferring the day of the actual take-over. And during the five years when nothing seemed settled, the Frenchmen at New Orleans dared to scheme to remain French.

The reception they gave Don Antonio de Ulloa, the first governor appointed by Spain, was less than gracious. Not that these Frenchmen in 1768 sought to preserve hard-won liberties or to gain them, as was soon to happen in the Anglo-American colonies. They were simply expressing disapproval of the exchange of one master for another. These New Orleanians had good trade relations with the French Caribbean and they feared the regulations for which Spain was notorious. And so this small group of colonial French rebel leaders armed both the German farmers outside of town and the recently arrived French Acadians, who had been transported by England from their homes in Nova Scotia because of their resistance to just such another land transfer.

The Louisiana Frenchmen, the Germans, and the Acadians forced the withdrawal of the governor amid general, if short-lived, rejoicing.

But if the Spanish dons were unhurried, they were also persistent. Soon a veritable armada, bearing 2,600 troops under a violent-tempered martinet of Irish descent named Don Alexander O'Reilly anchored off New Orleans, and the five principal French leaders were executed. Their names deserve to be remembered: Nicolas Chauvin de Lafrenière, Jean Baptiste Noyan, Pierre Caresse, Pierre Marquis and Joseph Milhet. If they were not martyrs to political freedom, they were pioneers in trying to achieve just such self-determination as the modern world has grown accustomed to expect.

The blood that was spilled brought order and accommodation. The Frenchman and the Spaniard in colonial Louisiana learned to live together. The Spanish took to the French cuisine and Creole belles. The French so admired the Spanish architecture that what we call the New Orleans French Quarter should really be known as the Spanish Quarter because it is so distinctly Iberian. And, yes, the Latin kinsmen had a common affinity for the sins of the flesh. While the bloodstreams were fusing to create probably the most attractive people of the new America, English-speaking Scots-Irish were following the Wilderness Road that Daniel Boone had blazed, to clear their corn patches in the forest and soon to seek outlets for their grain and whiskey and other produce by river to New Orleans and through that port to the eastern seaboard.

The needs of these Kaintucks would lead in 1803 to another land transfer which would be as distasteful at first to the Creoles as the one that was made in 1762.

For the red tribesmen of America, the Seven Years' War of unknown Europe produced results as personal as for the white men. During that war and the two years of preceding border warfare, Pontiac, the fierce and canny Ottawa chief of the Illinois country, remained loyal to France. In 1763 he united the Indians of the Upper Mississippi in a conspiracy against the English forts and trading posts, and British troops and colonials could not stay the rapid attacks. But the alliance collapsed and Pontiac's own siege of Detroit was a failure. Nonetheless, Pontiac's activities postponed as effectively the day of the English taking over Fort Chartres as did the Frenchmen's conspiracy delay Spanish imposition of authority at New Orleans. Not death by firing squad ended Pontiac's life, but the hand of an Indian assassin hired by a British trader. He was murdered at Cahokia in 1769.

England extended her dominion to the river's eastern bank, while Spain assumed command on the western side.

Above the Isle of Orleans, on the north shore of Bayou Manchac, the English soon established a fort and warehouse and felled trees to widen the waterway, hoping thereby to divert the Mississippi and its trade toward the English seaboard colonies. But the river itself sided with Spain, and England's plans came to nothing: for the timber, cut at the upper end of the bayou, was swept along on the spring flood to become a matted thicket of logs caught in the trees farther down.

More successful were the English colonials who had accepted land grants at Natchez as payment for their participation in the French and Indian War and who became prosperous planters on the rolling bluffs.

During the war years, a New Orleans trading firm formed by Gilbert de St. Maxent and Pierre Laclède Liguest, which had received the fur monopoly from France for the Missouri country, had planned to establish a trading post on the Mississippi's east bank near the protection of Fort Chartres, and Laclède went up to the fort by keelboat to scout a location. In February 1764, he sent his wife's son, Auguste Chouteau, and a party of workers across the river to clear land for the post on the west bank instead. Here was the first elevated land below the confluence of the Illinois and the Missouri rivers with the Mississippi. The little settlement, whose population was soon swelled by Upper River Frenchmen who preferred Spanish to English rule, was named St. Louis, for the patron saint of France. (In 1927, when a son of the river land, Charles Augustus Lindbergh, became the first man to fly the Atlantic alone in his *Spirit of St. Louis*, the French felt they shared in this achievement through the name of his plane.)

England's tenure along the river was short. Freed from France's inhibiting power by the ending of the war, the Atlantic seaboard colonists turned their attention to other accounts and in 1775 began the revolution which brought them freedom from overseas domination. In the name of the colonists, George Rogers Clark captured the English posts of Kaskaskia and Cahokia,

*Near Greenville, Mississippi*

thereby assuring American, rather than British, ownership of the western lands north of the Ohio.

In support of the revolution because it was against England, young Governor Bernardo de Gálvez of New Orleans seized Fort Manchac and the English towns of Baton Rouge and Natchez. For Gálvez's share in the war, Britain's West Florida became Spanish, and Spain's holdings on the east bank of the Mississippi were thereby extended northward. A subsequent diplomatic tussle between the United States and Spain ended when the border was set at the thirty-first parallel, making Tory Natchez an American town.

But the American settlers on the river were at the mercy of Spain in their trade with the world. Whoever controlled the Isle of Orleans could slow the commerce of part of the United States. Kentucky, the first state with the river as a border, had entered the Union in 1792 as the fifteenth state. Its hunters and farmers and woodsmen needed the river for a highway, as did those in Tennessee, which had achieved statehood in 1796. New Orleans was vital as a port wherein to deposit their goods, free of Spanish tax, until their shipments could be reloaded for Charleston, Philadelphia, New York, Boston, or the world. American treaties with Spain which promised the young United States

the right of deposit and freedom of navigation on the Mississippi were precarious. But when weak Spain retroceded Louisiana to Napoleon's vigorous France and even dared to withhold the right of deposit, the westerners saw war as the only recourse.

President Thomas Jefferson, however, in 1803 dispatched James Monroe to Paris as minister plenipotentiary to join the American minister there, Robert R. Livingston, in trying to obtain reaffirmation of America's right to free navigation of the river and, if possible, to purchase the Isle of Orleans. Additionally, they were instructed to try to buy West Florida so the entire east bank would be American. From this quest for free navigation of the Mississippi River came the serendipity of the Louisiana Purchase.

During the negotiations Monroe laughingly proposed, without thought of being taken seriously, that perhaps Napoleon would like to pay off claims of some American ship owners by turning Louisiana over to the United States. To his consternation, Napoleon replied that he would! The ministers had not been authorized to make such a deal, but they seized the opportunity and agreed to the purchase, which a hesitant Congress finally endorsed.

But no American had yet explored the

country acquired in the purchase. Indians and traders knew the Missouri as a waterway to the West, but no white man had discovered its length or reached the Pacific by land so far north of Mexico. Even before the Louisiana Purchase, President Jefferson had wanted to know what lay west of the Mississippi, and now Lewis and Clark were in winter quarters near St. Louis, waiting to find out after the spring thaws.

Their boats left the Mississippi on May 14, 1804, going up the Missouri, the Mississippi's longest tributary, to its headwaters in the Rockies. The members of the expedition then rode Shoshoni ponies until they reached a tributary of the Columbia, which they descended to the Pacific. These explorers unfolded a land that stretched to the Pacific and initiated a migration westward that thousands of Americans would follow. Two years and four months after their departure, Lewis and Clark were back at St. Louis with the information which made tiny St. Louis the center for westward expansion.

The $15 million Louisiana Purchase bought the land west of the river. It did not include the last Spanish-held territory on the east bank.

Above New Orleans, West Florida like the muzzle of a pistol was connected with the butt which was Spain's East Florida. But the spirit of West Florida was American. Into that small stretch of river land had moved English-speaking farmers on the invitation of Spain, which for once had relaxed her policies against non-Catholics. Her hope was that by permitting these strange Protestants to settle on the buffer strip, she might build a colony for the protection of Florida. But Spanish restrictions, no matter how loosely administered, were still Spanish and galling. In 1812 the dissenting Scots-Irish rode their ponies at dawn into the Spanish fort at Baton Rouge by mingling with the milking cows, and the horsemen became the first mounted force in history to take a fortified European encampment. They ran a white Masonic star on a blue background up the flagpole, and for ten weeks the West Florida Republic, the only independent republic ever created along the river's banks, maintained its integrity. In the end American troops from New Orleans drew the small, independent country to the American bosom.

And so, as in 1762, the river again ran through a valley owned by a single nation. The role of the Mississippi as an international boundary had come to an end. Henceforth along the entire river, from the west bank or the east, Americans could look across the Mississippi and see only America. At least that's what the maps said; Sauks and Foxes and Illinois and Sioux and Choctaws and Cherokees were not included in the treaties made in Europe. But possession of the Mississippi was not yet settled.

On Harman Blennerhassett's island in the Ohio, Aaron Burr, third vice-president of the United States, had turned burning eyes toward the gold mines of Mexico and envisioned an empire for himself. At New Orleans, Gen. James Wilkinson, commander of American forces in the West who had bent a willing ear to Burr in St. Louis, awaited his coming—but whether to assist him or seize him is not clear. Burr's arrest for treason a few miles back from Natchez had put an end to whatever the scheme had been.

Only then could Gov. W. C. C. Claiborne get on with the Americanization of the Orleans

Territory. Here were Spaniards and Frenchmen, and Creoles descended from both; Germans, whose ancestors were among the first to come; Acadians, on the bayous; black men, as indigenous now as the masters for whom they labored; colored men and women, freed by their fathers; and recent arrivals, the French-speaking San Domingan refugees. On all of these a new tongue and a new law and a new constitution had yet to be grafted. The very presence of thousands of eastern seaboard Americans who had flocked to Louisiana since the Purchase added to the tensions of the river country in transition.

No wonder then that Britain, late in the War of 1812, thought the rich city at the mouth of the river ripe for taking, a conquest which would assure her a piece of the valley in the peace treaty even then being negotiated at Ghent.

In December 1814, Maj. Gen. Sir Edward Pakenham, brother-in-law of the Duke of Wellington, with an armada of fifty of the British navy's finest ships and 20,000 soldiers and sailors arrived in the swampy bayou country below New Orleans.

To meet them, Andrew Jackson of Tennessee, charged by the government with the protection of the Gulf ports and the Mississippi Valley, gathered a force consisting of 884 U.S. regulars and every able-bodied man in the city, whatever his origin or condition—Creole, Acadian, American, Negro, Indian, pirate, San Domingan. And down the river floated a fleet of flatboats packed with fringe-shirted Kentuckians and Tennesseans, with their long rifles which turned out to outrange the arms of the British.

On the eighth of January, 1815, Andy's men, 2,350 of them, took their stations behind hastily thrown up breastworks on the city side of the shallow, ten-foot-wide Rodriguez Canal, on the plain of Chalmette. The Jackson line extended not much more than a mile, from the river to a cypress swamp. The British Highlanders and other regulars had to march across the open field, facing the incredibly accurate sharpshooters

*New Orleans, Louisiana*

from Tennessee and awaiting the arrival of fascines—bundles of cane—which no one had yet ordered to be thrown onto the slippery canal floor.

The battle, which began at 7:00 A.M., was all but over by 2:00. By then General Pakenham and Maj. Gen. Sir Patrick Giles lay dead, and the British had lost 2,057 officers and men at the Rodriguez breastworks. The American losses were astonishing: 6 killed and 7 wounded. By the end of the month the British sailed away, leaving behind a people more united because they had fought a common foe.

Before the epochal battle, to assure that no British forces could attack his rear by water, Jackson ordered Bayou Manchac filled in. So ended for all time the Isle of Orleans, which had changed hands so often. Perhaps here was a symbol that no further treaties describing transfers of river land from Western power to Western power would be written.

But if external threats were over, internal problems remained.

The land hunger of the settlers pressing westward in the Upper River country and up and down the Lower River, in search of new cotton fields, brought Indian wars and Indian treaties and the enforced removal of the original Americans to new hunting grounds across the Mississippi.

Portentous for the white man's settlement of the Upper River was an Indian war which bears the name of Black Hawk, the heroic Sauk chief. Black Hawk's fault lay in his love of his independence and the law of his forebears. Both stood in the way of a new freedom and a new code and both were doomed. He was as great an American as ever trod our land and he loved it as his own words attest: "Rock River was a beautiful country; I loved my towns, my cornfields, and the home of my people. I fought for it."

Born in 1767 at the great Sauk village on Rock River, two miles above where it enters the Mississippi, Black Hawk fought American expansion almost to the day of his death, arguing that a treaty signed at St. Louis in 1804 which surrendered Sauk lands east of the river was negotiated by drunken Indians who were not empowered to act as envoys. Until 1829 he sought the assistance of England to help halt the white men who were crowding into his people's ancestral hunting lands, even ahead of the provisions in the treaty under which they claimed the right to settle. Despairing of aid from Canada and encouraged by a Winnebago medicine man, Black Hawk and his Indian allies threatened war to block the newcomers. But Gen. Edmund P. Gaines from the small fist of Fort Armstrong on Rock Island forced the resolute chief to withdraw west of the Mississippi, where he would have remained save for the hunger which brought him and his people back to plant the fields they had left on the Illinois side. The white militia panicked and their too precipitate action resulted in the retaliation of scalpings and war whoops and terror on the frontier. Volunteers—among them a young man from the Sangamon named Abraham Lincoln—were mobilized. But it took regulars as well as militia to defeat the red men fighting for their homeland. At the Bad Axe River in July 1832, Black Hawk's warriors were slaughtered—women and children as ruthlessly as were the men, although a flag of truce was flying. Black Hawk himself was taken as prisoner to Prairie du Chien, a short distance upriver from the mining areas of Galena and Dubuque, where hot lead was poured down the height of tall shot towers to form the round balls for rifles and muskets which tumbled Indians and animals alike. In time Black Hawk was returned to Iowa in the custody of Keokuk, his rival and a friend of the Americans. By the treaty of September 1832, all the Sauk and Fox lands in eastern Iowa were ceded to the United States.

Peace came then to the northern frontier and with it the filling up of the Upper River's prairie and forest lands by Germans, Norwegians, Swedes, men from Maine and men from New York, all seeking to create a new world for themselves. Their sons, and even some of them, would

give and take American lives in the terrible bloodletting of 1861–65.

And before that, the towns below St. Louis would know the beat of drums and a rallying of soldiers who would steam up the Red River or ferry across to wooded trails or embark at New Orleans, to fight for Texas freedom or against Mexico.

In April 1861, men on river steamboats carried to little lumber towns of the Upper River, to isolated plantations in the lower reaches, the tragic news which telegraph had brought to the cities: A nation was at war with itself.

The Upper River states were strongly pro-Union. But already Mississippi and Louisiana had declared themselves out of the Union; Arkansas would secede in May; Tennessee would vote on secession for a second time in June; Kentucky was in doubt; and pro-Confederacy feeling ran high in Missouri. Again the Mississippi coursed seaward through lands owning different allegiances.

For the Confederacy, the river was the lifeline to cotton and corn and manpower in the states which it bordered or traversed, and to Texas as well. For the Union, control of the Mississippi would mean blocking the South from

access to vital supplies and men; and once all the Lower River lands had been strangled, the Confederacy could be annihilated in detail.

That danger was not as apparent to the Confederacy in the first months of the war as it would become later. Thousands of fighting men from the Deep South entrained for the defense of the capital, Richmond, Virginia. Although U.S.S. *Brooklyn* stood off the river's mouth and enforced a blockade which soon disrupted commerce and inflated prices in the river towns, the Mississippi seemed safe, far behind the Confederate lines which stretched from the Cumberland Gap through Nashville and Bowling Green to a point near New Madrid.

Not for a year would a shooting war actually come to the Lower River's banks in the form of Farragut's fleet and Porter's mortars.

Meanwhile, at headquarters for the Western District in St. Louis, Maj. Gen. John C. Frémont filled steamboats-become-transports with farm-boy volunteers from Minnesota, Iowa, Wisconsin, Illinois, and the other midwestern states, and sent them off to Cairo—Cairo farther south than Richmond itself, Cairo which the Union must prevent from becoming northern gateway for southern guerrillas, Cairo which would become staging area for the Union's forces in their conquest of the river.

And to Cairo, General Frémont sent Ulysses

S. Grant, former West Pointer who had not amounted to much in the army and who had been clerking in his brothers' store at Galena, up a tiny Mississippi River tributary in Illinois.

And to Cairo came also the Turtles, strange-looking ironclad gunboats designed—and many of them built—by a river-engineering genius from St. Louis named James B. Eads. They would protect the Union navy's flotilla, which was braced by 500 saltwater sailor boys and by thousands of landlubbers from the mid-continent's farms.

Farragut. Grant. Eads's ironclads. And in the end, hunger.

The Union plan was to strike at both ends of the Mississippi, take control of the river, move east, and then dismember the Confederacy section by section.

To protect the Federal forces from attack from Kentucky was Grant's first responsibility. His initial sortie from Cairo to Belmont, a river landing in Missouri across the river from Confederate-fortified Columbus, proved a disaster when his men celebrated victory too soon and had to flee to their waiting transports.

His next move would bring him fame and the assurance that no Confederate army could attack his rear down the Tennessee or the Mississippi. Here was the first major engagement of the new amphibious war. With his troops on transports, and gunboats going ahead up the Ohio, Grant's forces entered the Tennessee. On February 6, 1862, after a battering by the Federal fleet, Fort Henry controlling the Tennessee surrendered. Ten days later at the Cumberland, Grant and his upriver boys forced the "unconditional surrender" of Fort Donelson, and the initials of the stocky officer's name took on new meaning, and he was promoted to general.

Leaving the boats behind, Grant swept southward across Tennessee and was not stopped until Gen. Albert Sidney Johnston attacked unexpectedly at Shiloh. Johnston bled to death from a wound on the first evening, and thousands of southern and northern boys died in the bloody two-day battle. For the next four months the two armies sparred cautiously. On the Mississippi the gunboats and Gen. John Pope's army took Columbus, New Madrid, and Island No. 10, and the Union navy fought and defeated a smaller force of the Confederate navy near Memphis to make possible the occupation of both Memphis and Fort Pillow above it.

Meanwhile, to the south, New Orleans shivered in the spring rains as Farragut pulled his gunboats across the silted river bar and sailed upstream with his fleet of seventeen wooden vessels and Porter's ironclad mortar boats. Between Farragut and the city stood two ancient forts, one on either side of the river and connected now by a chain laid across the channel and by a defensive fleet of nine vessels. The city depended on the forts to stop any invasion up the river from the Gulf. For five days and nights Porter's gunboats bombarded the forts. Then, in the early moonless hours of April 24, Farragut's fleet steamed under the guns of the forts and through a break in the chain. Three of the Confederate boats fought valiantly; the rest were ignominiously beached and scuttled.

Though the Confederate forts behind him had not surrendered, Farragut anchored off New Orleans on April 25, and on May 1 Gen. Ben Butler led the Union forces into the city which would be held fifteen years by Union troops.

Farragut continued upriver, taking Bayou Lafourche, the important waterway to the Gulf; Baton Rouge, with its arsenal; and Natchez, which accepted the inevitable and surrendered. Then he headed for a rendezvous with flag officer Charles Henry Davis and the gunboats which had achieved victory at Memphis.

There could be no clean sweep of the river so long as Vicksburg and its batteries controlling river traffic remained in Confederate hands. And soon it became apparent that the city so high on the bluff required more than bombardment from the river alone. The unsuccessful attack was stopped. Not for a year would Vicksburg fall.

The terrain favored the defenders. Opposite

the little town, the river made a tight horseshoe bend toward the city to lap at the base of the 230-foot bluff. Batteries on the bluff would be trained on any boats in the river. Lowlands in the bend and all down the west bank would hamper any troop movements in that section. Eight miles upstream the Yazoo entered the river through swampy backwaters.

In the fall of 1862 Grant planned to approach the city from the east while Gen. William Tecumseh Sherman attacked from the north. Sherman reached Chickasaw Bayou north of Vicksburg late in December and attacked futilely, not knowing that Grant's plan had gone awry. A Confederate raid on Holly Springs, Mississippi, had destroyed his supplies stockpiled there for the campaign, and he had retired to Memphis to reassemble materiel and plan again.

In January Grant was ready to move.

The Western Flotilla transported his three army corps from Memphis to Milliken's Bend, some twenty miles above Vicksburg. Grant, on his headquarters steamboat, the *Magnolia*, pulled on his pipe and studied the maps and charts. How get his troops around and up to the high ground back of Vicksburg? He couldn't transport them safely past the batteries and so down to a landing below fortified Vicksburg and Grand Gulf. How else?

If a ditch were cut across the peninsula pointed at Vicksburg, the Mississippi might cooperate by tearing through and scouring out a passage for transports. Thus could he bring his men in safety to a position below the city. But the plan didn't work. The engineers' knowledge of the river was scanty and the Mississippi ignored such an enticing, hopeful passage. If the levee on the west bank were pierced to let river water flow toward Lake Providence, an ancient bed of the Mississippi, and other passages then deepened, the transports might make their way through to the Red River and enter the Mississippi above Port Hudson, held by the Confederates on Louisiana's east bank. But the entry from river to lake proved too narrow, tree-choked, and

finally impossible for the transports to use.

On the east bank there had once been an opening called Yazoo Pass, now closed by levees. Through this, small steamboats had chugged to bring provisions to backcountry plantations. If the levee were broached, certainly the gunboats could go by way of the Coldwater, and down the Tallahatchie to where the Yalobusha met it to form the Yazoo, and so reach the bluffs well behind Vicksburg. Unable to maneuver, and tailing each other through this narrow waterway, the Turtles arrived at Greenwood, where the batteries of a fort constructed of cotton bales stopped them. Dragged to safety stern first because they didn't have room to turn around, the ironclads obviously were not going to be able to get through this passage either.

Finally, there was Steele's Bayou, which entered the Yazoo five miles from its mouth. If Porter's gunboats could negotiate Steele's Bayou into Black Bayou and Deer Creek and Rolling Fork into the Sunflower, they could reach the Yazoo above the Confederate fortification on that river. Porter soon found himself impacted in a swampy forest while Confederate snipers from the banks picked off his men. Finally, Sherman's troops came to rescue the hapless expedition.

From where he was, there was no way to get east of Vicksburg except by one last desperate way. Grant took it.

Transports would have to run the gauntlet of those Vicksburg batteries. Not transports loaded with men, but transports which, once safely below the river redoubt, would be available to pick up and carry across the Mississippi the troops who had marched down the west side to the east bank. And the troops would have to build a road across the mire of the peninsula and march to where they would be crossed.

On the night of April 16 Grant's gunboats successfully ran the batteries, and a few nights later the wooden transports succeeded in getting by. Only one was sunk and that, unfortunately, was the one loaded with medical supplies. On

April 30 the Federal troops crossed the river to Bruinsburg, ten miles below Grand Gulf, and now Grant was where he wanted to be: "on high ground on the same side of the river with the enemy."

Taking Port Gibson, which, belying its name, was not on the Mississippi but near a crossroads leading to Jackson and Vicksburg, Grant hurried himself to take Grand Gulf from the rear.

In mid-May the Federal forces took Raymond, southwest of Mississippi's state capital of Jackson, and then Jackson itself. Gen. John Pemberton, who had come out of Vicksburg to their assistance, was driven back into the city. The boys of the Upper River dug trenches around the city that was so vital to the Confederate cause, and the long and exhausting siege of Vicksburg was on.

For days the city resisted while irreplaceable provisions dwindled. Soon even rats became delectable. And then there was nothing left but hollow, desolate hunger.

On the morning of July 4, 1863, General Pemberton surrendered the city to General Grant, and the bloodied slopes of Vicksburg became in time a cross-studded military cemetery. Port Hudson held out a few days longer under conditions of at least as great starvation as at Vicksburg. But by August President Lincoln could write: "The Father of Waters again goes unvexed to the sea."

Lincoln's Emancipation Proclamation in January had declared freedom for all slaves behind Union lines. Now forts and cities on the river were garrisoned by black troops headed by white officers, while the seasoned Union troops marched east to accomplish the destruction of the Confederacy.

During April of 1864 occurred one of those horrors the passions of war sometimes unleash. A raid by Nathan Bedford Forrest's men on Union-garrisoned Fort Pillow turned into carnage when Forrest's men, yelling "Kill the niggers! Kill the niggers!" overran the fort.

When the raid was over a majority of the Negro defenders had been slain, whether before or after surrender was agreed to is not clear.

Then in a year the isolated farms and towns which had heard of peace learned of another great national tragedy. Flags at half-mast on the gunboats on the river told the river folk that President Lincoln was dead.

This is not solely a history of the white man on the river: It concerns all men, and men and the river.

Today on the Lower River, where black men often outnumber white, the blacks are finding opportunities and political rights savored but briefly by their forebears. These men are descendants of unwilling immigrants who, like the rest of immigrant America, shared in the development of the country and in the defense of the nation.

Muscles in black arms chopped the wild cane and turned the gummy sod. Black shoulders dragged heavy cotton sacks as they filled them with white bolls. Black backs bent to the oars of dispatch boats, and black arms stoked the steamboats that could not compete with railroads the black men had built through swamps and valleys. Black hands on wheelbarrows and shovels threw up the levees for protection of what they had helped create, including the hearths of their own cabin homes. Black fingers fashioned armoires, tables, chairs, beds, which are treasured heirlooms in the columned mansions built by skilled black artisans.

Under Bernardo de Gálvez, eighty free blacks helped the cause of American independence by active participation in the campaign against Fort Manchac and Baton Rouge; descendants of their white counterparts are members of the Daughters of the American Revolution. Under Andrew Jackson at New Orleans, 400 free men of color fought at the ramparts to save their country from the British. In every war since then, the United States has called on the black men of the river country along with the white, and never in greater percentage than in the Vietnam conflict. Black volunteer units for the Confederate army were turned down, but black troops from the East made the impossible assault on Port Hudson in Louisiana, held courageously at Fort Pillow which protected Federal navigation of the river, and took part in many another action. Black troops were major components of the army of occupation throughout the river country.

In the wake of the internecine war, the black majority elected black mayors and lesser officials and helped send black congressmen to Washington before Jim Crow came to perch on the American flag. There came then a hiatus and many black men left the Lower River valley to seek, but not always to find, a better future for themselves and their children. One of the worst race riots during World War I was the result of importation of black strikebreakers to East St. Louis, Illinois. But some blacks who remained in the land of their fathers were able to triumph within the system. Businessmen like Thomy Lafon, philanthropic with their wealth, endowed schools and other institutions. From New Orleans spread jazz, the creation of superb black musicians and the one distinctively American contribution to music.

The assassination of Martin Luther King, Jr., in Memphis in 1968 closed banks and government offices in a national day of mourning but helped open wider the gates of equal opportunity, not only to the black men of the river land but to black Americans everywhere.

Today the question asked by La Salle and Iberville, the great question of who would profit from the Mississippi Valley, seems at last to have been answered: America, and all Americans.

61

# Romance

If the history of the Mississippi Valley could be told in terms of nationalities, it might be simply said that the French were the claimants and colonizers, the Spaniards the rejecters of the opportunity to gain the wealth which they contradictorily had found to the south, the English the usurpers and conquerers, and the Anglo-Americans the settlers and nation builders. What is significant in terms of the nationalities and colonization is that most of the giants of the valley were Frenchmen—La Salle, Iberville, Bienville, Laclède—and later a dashing Spaniard, Bernardo de Gálvez, who married a Creole girl.

It is no oversimplification to say that whereas the Latins of France and of Spain came as soldiers and mercenaries and traders bent principally on making money, at least in the beginning, the men of the British Isles, with their genius for nationhood, came to stay. The lands that they accepted or preempted became the home places, as did those of other Nordics in the New World from Minnesota to Head of the Passes. This is the only way of looking at the valley with any certainty about the intent of its populators. In that light let us consider now some of the facts of history, remembering above all else the true story concerns the river itself.

It was not the adze and handsaw and hammer of the house builder that was the most meaningful American contribution. The French and the Spaniards of the early days built lovelier houses by far, such as Villa Louis, built in Prairie du Chien during the Astor fur-trading era. What the Americans who came to the river erected was an idea and an ideal which we can simplify with two abused words, human freedom. The Anglo-Americans brought to the land of European religious and political authority a hopefulness for man's future, a dream of independence in thought, behavior, and religion. Because they were what they were, the Anglo-Americans were the true validators of freedom in the valley of the Mississippi.

The people who live along the Mississippi belong primarily to certain groups of differing national origin, each having its principal locale in different reaches of the river. In the Upper River country we find the Scandinavians.

They came at first in a trickle, and then in an onrushing, more than 200,000 by midnineteenth century, seeking freedom and a future and a providing land. And these they found. They were the forebears of a Carl Sandburg, chanting American glory. They made a destined nation more certain of its destiny. They became

the spine of the Upper Mississippi, these horny-handed, tough Nordics who add greatness wherever they go.

In the Middle River country are descendants of the French, who met the German newcomers in peace.

Along the Lower River are the Scots-Irish, whose fathers flatboated from Kentucky and Tennessee to New Orleans and, returning by land, cleared new homesites on ground recently wrested by treaty from the Indians. And here, as elsewhere, the Irish, who came to the river towns from the potato crop failures of their native land. At Natchez and Baton Rouge are the descendants of Englishmen who came to terms with Spain or set their own terms, and the Creoles, who are persons of French and Spanish blood born on colonial soil. Alongside them are the progeny of John Law's Germans and other Germans who came later, fleeing the Old World in search of political freedom, and the Acadians, whose name was shortened to Cajun and who were Creoles too, though their first homes were in Nova Scotia.

Finally, below New Orleans, nearer the delta of a river which opens out to the world, a colorful mosaic has been formed, composed of Jugoslav and Italian and Malay and Chinese and Norwegian and Cajun, yes, and Anglo-American, so intertwined along the passes and bayous as almost to create a new race.

Those to come to the river included some people who had known the meaning of racial and religious persecution. Among these people were Jews who first sold their wares from the packs on their backs, and who were refugees from Spain and Portugal and Germany and Russia and Poland and wherever else they had been persecuted and murdered. Today the Jew of the South is not a Jew but a Southerner. Only one of many of them need be cited here. His name was Judah P. Benjamin. His plantation home was Belle Chasse, just below New Orleans on the river's right bank, and he became secretary of war of the Confederacy.

Binding all of the river peoples together as a catalyst and threat—the really dissimilar riverman, as far as appearance goes—is the black man in whose veins runs the blood of many of the rest, just as in the veins of some of the rest runs the black man's blood, though it is denied. One also must count the sons of the Indians of the river country, though their lineage and their hopes alike run thin.

In 1858 a Louisiana cartographer named Adrienne Persac drew and hand-colored for reproduction a remarkable map which he entitled *Plantations on the Mississippi River from Natchez to New Orleans*. It faithfully depicts the river and shows to scale on each side the plantations which abutted each other all the way downriver from just above Natchez to just below New Orleans. In the corners of the map are jewellike scenes of New Orleans, Baton Rouge, a sugar plantation, and a cotton plantation, each as seen from the river. On each plat Persac printed the names of the plantation owners. Those names survive now in proof of the families that once dominated the Lower River. Not all of them today are those of wealthy men but there are almost none whose bearers stand without respect. Among the owners of sugar plantations are honored French names—Lavergne, Lacour, Poché, Ledoux, Lacoste, Hébert, Gaudet, Bringier; and German names—Webre, Buehler, going back to the early days of settlement; but only a scattering of Spanish names—few Spaniards came as farmers or planters, because their roles were those of military and political representatives of Spain.

On the map's roster of river planters are also inscribed the owners who were predominantly English and Scots-Irish, as well as the native-born Americans who came from the western rivers and the eastern seaboard to find their future in the valley after 1764 and after the later Louisiana Purchase. This was the restless, surging free citizenry of a new nation-in-the-building whose people were not content to stay where they had been or remain what they were

COTTON PLANTATION

SUGAR PLANTATION

BATON ROUGE

NEW ORLEANS

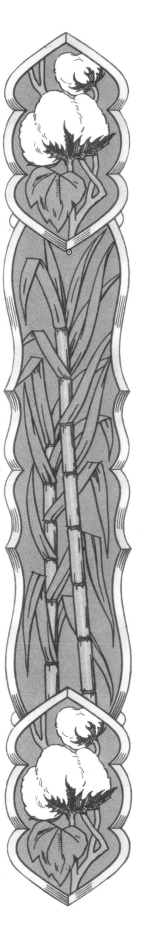

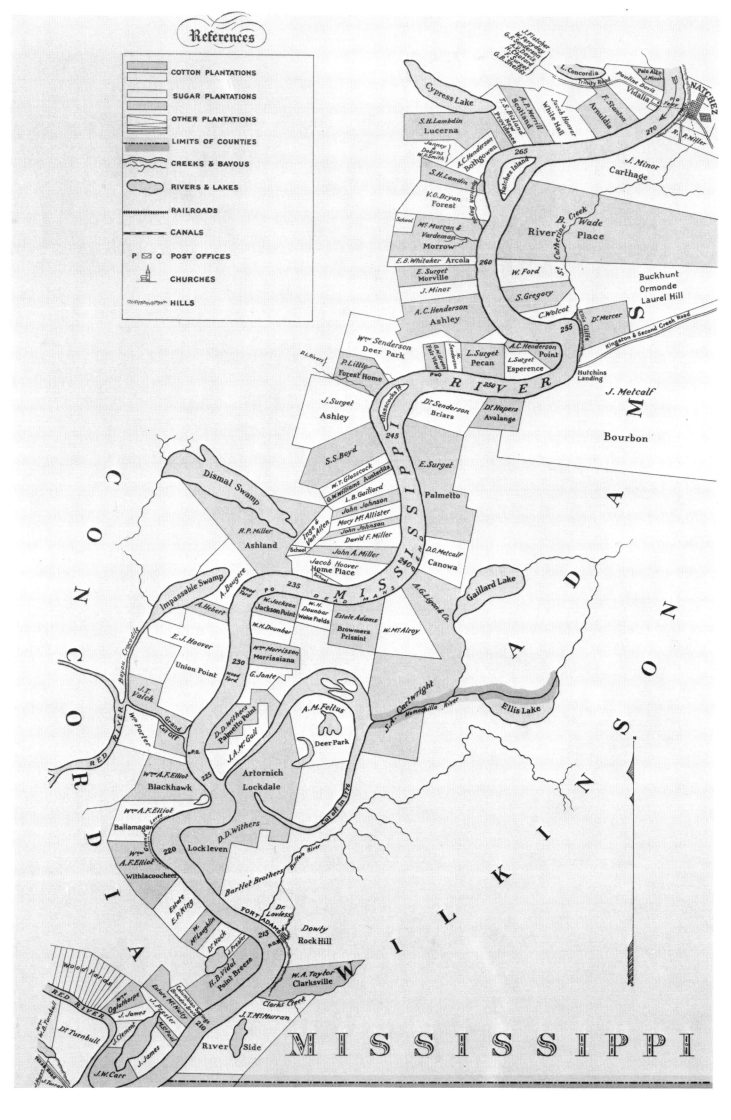

*Adrienne Persac map, "Plantations on the Mississippi River from Natchez to New Orleans, 1858"*

or be restricted to the lot of their fathers—the Hendersons, the Dunbars, the Stantons, the Gays, the McCalls, the Perkinses, the Mc-Laughlins, the Uptons, the Barrows, the Claibornes. The spirit of the English yeomen still whispers to the heirs of Magna Carta that this is our own, our native land.

From Minnesota to St. Louis, ours is also a Nordic land. As for myself, I like these Americans better than any other people who live along the river, and let praise be sung to the old solid virtues that are mocked at by a new America and are more honored in the breach than in the observance. These are the scions of peasant farmers, of hog raisers and cow milkers of the European western lands. They do their own work as much as they can and they don't go in for black tenants as do their fellow tillers of the soil downstream. They are the quarter-section farmers whose sons populated and made great the universities of the Middle West. They have an unchanging quality which I like and envy. There are no more prosperous or better Americans than these.

In the southeast corner of the once ferociously debated lands of Missouri, hard against the river, lies the "bootheel," whose people think of themselves as southern and live like the most southern of southerners, arguing states' rights. They are cotton planters in an old tradition and unwilling to accept political or economic change. For all their stiff backs, they are generous, loyal to friends, and proud of a tradition they refuse to let vanish. I like them if only because they are akin to the country neighbors and fellow townsmen I have known so long.

Below the bootheel country lie the cotton fields of Tennessee on the east bank and then the flat delta lands of Arkansas and Mississippi, the bluffs of proud Natchez, and the hills that rise from the bluffs to Baton Rouge, though not unbrokenly. This is the country of greatest black density. It is also Anglo-Saxon country, its people so like as like in their build and facial qualities as to look, almost all of them, like brothers and sisters. They are a hot-tempered lot, with much narrowness and false pride to them, and they are not people to monkey with. I would say that southerners, among them myself, could live without their shortcomings while clinging rightfully to their manifold virtues. They too were sired by the first to come here. Their heirs and they will not be uprooted nor, for a long time to come, will their attitudes be greatly amended. It is hard to change farm folk anywhere, and here the presence of the Negro makes for a sick solidarity among the whites.

The people of the valley are a religiously heterogeneous folk today, with the spires of the Lutheran churches, the Baptist, the Presbyterian, the Methodist, the Episcopalian, and latterly the Pentecostal sects pointing into the river sky, along with those of the Roman Catholic. Until the Louisiana Purchase the Roman Catholic faith was predominant by law and by heritage. Until then, no Protestant service, from baptism to burial, could legally be held in Spain's land along the river. But such rites were performed anyway. And while Protestantism was not welcome in the Mississippi Valley under France and Spain, as has ever been the way with Protestants they persisted in their faith and spread it. Whatever Rome or Madrid or Paris might have ordained, the Protestants survived and prospered spiritually. Some of them paid religious and civil lip service to Catholic Spain in return for land grants, but they clung to their Protestant faith.

When the Louisiana Purchase made of the river a bridge rather than a barrier, land and fortune seekers in the thousands floated to the new frontier on the Mississippi, bringing their Bibles with them into a valley whose unofficial tolerance had been sustained by Creoles who would brook no Inquisition or hairshirted rigidity. But the easygoing faith of the frontier was the target of early evangelists—the most colorful of whom, Lorenzo Dow, preached hell and damnation in the Natchez area in the first decade of the nineteenth century. Had such men

*Joseph Smith house, Nauvoo, Illinois*

had their way, the river folk would have been as intolerant as any in the New World. But the river gives windows on the world, and through them blows the breeze of tolerance which cools the perfervid imaginings of those who see hell in every pleasure.

Lorenzo Dow, to yesterday's river baptismal ceremonies, to today's sad denial . . . .

These are too long vanished: the riverside baptismal ceremonies, the exhorting preachers and elders, the ecstatic saved who have come to Jesus, the fish fries where the white folks were once gladly welcomed. Our land is different now. I mourn what has gone and I pray that somehow it will return, not in values that equate superior and inferior but those which give to all of us our own unique places in the sun.

But there can be no challenge to the statement that, however significant the impact of Protestantism in the valley of the Mississippi, the Roman Catholic church has left and keeps alive an enduring and memorable heritage of quietude and, after the first brutal years of conquest, an indelible expression of man's love for his brother. The tolerance of a New Orleans stands in singular contrast to the backwoods fundamentalist Protestantism of the hinterlands. The Catholic missionary priests entered the valley believing that they were men with an inspired mission, and holy in great part they remained. Almost no community in the middle or lower valley would be what it is were it not for Roman Catholicism. Even an unbelievably just community like my own, Greenville, which numerically is one-sidedly Protestant, bears the singular imprint of its greatest son, William Alexander Percy—poet, philosopher, philanthropist, Catholic humanist—who was born into the Church, abandoned it (but not its principles) in his mature lifetime, and returned to it on his deathbed. The river towns are the tolerant towns of middle America and I believe this is true because of the Catholic church itself. For an imbedded spirit of hate you must look elsewhere.

But among a minority, a converse religious and social inquietude haunted the Mississippi River long after the departure of France and Spain. In the river city of Alton in Illinois is a monument to a murdered martyr to freedom of the press. His name was Elijah P. Lovejoy. In 1837 he was lynched in this town, which was then made up principally of southerners, because he spoke out in his abolitionist newspaper for human freedom.

And farther up the river the town of Nauvoo, home for a time for Joseph Smith and Brigham Young, was quitted in 1846 by the Mormons who had made of it within six years the showplace of Illinois. Rather than suffer longer the intolerance of their neighbors who had slaughtered their leaders, threatened their lives, and prevented peaceful use of the land they had made their own, the Latter-Day Saints sacrificed the creation of their hands—their temple, their buildings, and their homes—and, abandoning them in one of the most significantly American of all American migrations, sought religious freedom in a far distant Promised Land across their own Sinai.

The epic of the Mormons crossing the river and wending their way by oxcart and by wagon and even by pushcarts, for which the men were the beasts of burden, fills perhaps the noblest peacetime page in American history.

And there is a latter-day infamy. Its exponents call themselves—in diminishing number—members of the Ku Klux Klan, taking the organization's name from a once honorable post-Civil-War resistance movement in the South. The mental and moral filth of the Ku Klux Klan still smirches the flag of the Confederacy, which it traduces.

It is no happenstance that so many aspects of the river and its people have been or could have been the grist for a book, for they comprise the truths and the legends of a frontier. They are the challenges to an olden, more civilized New World. They are the doings of puny creatures who did not know that they were puny or that the Mississippi would brook no master. Only it did.

What I am setting down here, from memories and talk heard at a grandmother's knee, has mostly to do with frontier folk, in adversity, in war, and in a peace which stood only for the change in the enemy from man to nature. There is no end to those tales.

But I want to tell of a handful of French Canadians who lived almost like Indians and who were known as *coureurs de bois*. These frequenters of the forest defied church and state for more than a century as America's first revolutionaries. They opened the Mississippi Valley to settlement, which they themselves disliked, and to commerce—but only because of the *louis d'or* that it brought them, to be tossed away in the trading posts or at the proud little cities of Quebec and Montreal. What I like most about these wild Canadians is that they paddled against the current without knowing whence the current came. I like them for their independence in all matters.

To the despair of the Récollet priests and the Jesuit fathers and later the Spanish Capuchins, the *coureurs de bois* married or, more often, simply mated with the comely girls of the Illinois and the Natchez and the Choctaw and the other tribes which they encountered. When they tired of the sometimes martial discipline of the river settlements, these men simply took to the woods, usually to stay. The story of the *coureurs de bois* deserves as much telling as that of the English-speaking frontiersmen who streamed westward from the Atlantic seaboard.

And with the *coureurs de bois* should be recognized the first white women of the lower valley, the saucy maids of Paris's Salpêtrière, a sort of penitential and corrective home for fallen young females caught while plying their profession, and the *casquettes*, maidens of decent peasant stock who came with their tiny dowry trunks in search of husbands. They married and their children populated Louisiana and the colony was the better for it; but as a cynical latter-day historian has observed, it is strange that none of today's Creole aristocrats claim descent from the loins of the Salpêtrières, who obviously must have been regrettably infertile.

Then the seaboard American colonists came, trickling small and slowly at first, like the Mississippi at its source, and then they came like the tumultuous surging of the river in a swollen spring.

Of all the neo-barbarians of the river, I like to think most about the flatboatmen who, like Mike Fink, a legend among these legends, were called half alligator and half horse. These were the demijohn guzzlers, the eye gougers and groin kickers and rib butters, wielders of Bowie knives and short lengths of timber. They were the free spenders who took their flatboats apart in New Orleans and sold the timbers at the waterfront. When they had spent what they made from their voyage and the lumber, they set out overland, by the Natchez Trace, for Mississippi and northern Alabama and Tennessee and Kentucky and backwoods Virginia.

Not all of them made it. For there were other pirates in the valley besides the corsairs of the river—outlaws who would rob and murder a man, slit open his belly, fill the cavity with rock or gravel, and toss the violated body into a tributary.

As for the river pirates, their lair was in the caves and at the wooded base of shadowing bluffs, from which they could pounce on flatboats or keelboats as they floated round a bend or when they tied up to the bank for nighttime safety. The Chouteau fur men knew how to beat them at their game. The boats which would normally be sent from St. Louis one by one, loaded high with the fur company's buffalo hides and deer and beaver and fox and otter and muskrat pelts, were held back in the spring of 1788 until a flotilla of ten boats was ready to go downstream. The waiting pirates then learned the feel of buckshot and of rifle ball and the danger in their game in an epic confrontation which they had not expected.

*Natchez Under the Hill*

The flatboatmen made prosperous the bordellos and grog shops and gaming halls of New Orleans and St. Louis, to say nothing of the pawnshop owners, and the medical quacks who were specialists of the pox. But no one ever has had more fun than those roaring buckos of the Mississippi River.

And though they would not have recognized the fact, they were blood brothers of the gentleman killers of the dueling oaks and the dueling grounds across the river from Natchez who maimed and slew also, but with a lethal decorum which Mike would have considered a waste of time and talent.

And if they didn't keep their money, they kept in business many a light of love of the river towns' bordellos and cabaret girl and bar and gaming house operator. They were principally responsible for New Orleans' lasting reputation for convivial sin, which after all is something.

Maybe you once trudged behind and later fought Treasure Island's Long John Silver. If this is so, you will sign up with the pirates of the river's delta and its bayous; for New Orleans still elaborates the stories of Jean and Pierre Lafitte, the Creole brothers who smuggled and who boarded small merchant vessels, and who were very much respected in New Orleans, where they operated a blacksmith's shop as an unneeded cover. One of their lieutenants, a one-time artilleryman of Napoleon named Dominique You, served with distinction at the Battle of New Orleans. He is buried in an ancient cemetery, St. Louis No. 1, in a vault above ground as was the custom in swampy lands, and on his headstone is a Masonic emblem. There must be a rare story behind this man.

Or if you prefer a different kind of real-life swashbuckler, take the filibusters and other plotters of revolution who overthrew Latin American governments and set up new ones, ran wild for fat pay over what they derisively called banana republics, and joined up with one side or the other in the republics themselves—and always for money and the hell of it. They plotted their revolutions in hotels and whorehouses and even the homes of shadowy, rich men who backed them for financial reasons. Many a man who hunched over a mug or double toddy in the back parlor of some popular madam's establishment and argued how best to take Nicaragua or Mexico City died on the way, before he ever saw his objective. They were heady, trigger-happy, and indifferent, most of them, to right or wrong, and they left to North America a legacy of Latin hate and contempt which has not yet been dissipated.

Their kind was also recruited in New Orleans for a better and more desperate purpose. The defenders of the Alamo who died almost to the last man were filibusters largely recruited in New Orleans and, though they were gathered from all over the country and Europe, they sailed up-river to the Red and walked across Louisiana to Texas and from there to doom in a San Antonio presidio with the bugle notes of the *degüello*, the no-quarter call, shrilling in their ears.

Other flashes of color are less ominous or blood-bathed, such as the tales of the latter-day Norsemen, whose forebears were almost certainly the European discoverers of North America, and whose fathers fought against Indians and frozen nature and the South's defenders of slavery. Perhaps the story of the Scandinavian farmers and dairymen of the Upper Mississippi is the most American of them all. And if you think of them as placid, docile folk, read the inscribed names of the dead from Wisconsin and Illinois and Minnesota on the monuments in the federal cemetery at Vicksburg. Almost all of them are Norwegian or Swedish or Danish or German. And from these solid folk there soared forty years ago one who came not to be listed among the phlegmatic and the careful. His name is Charles Lindbergh.

What is now left for us are those two hardy perennials of the romantic river—New Orleans's Mardi Gras and the French Quarter. It's enough to say that despite commercialization, Mardi Gras is the most vivid and generously abandoned celebration on the North American continent and few of us who for years have masked and made merry at Mardi Gras would change anything. More than any other facet, Mardi Gras is New Orleans. So is the entire carnival season that begins traditionally with Twelfth Night and ends officially at the midnight before the beginning of the Lenten season.

And what new can be added to the saga of the French Quarter—the original city that is set off today by vital architectural restoration, and is as residentially desirable as it was scorned when I first returned to New Orleans as a cub reporter. The five-room furnished Quarter apartment for which another young reporter and I, both of us still unmarried, paid $22.50 a month rents today for $250, unfurnished. The *spumone* which was a nickel a block is a quarter now. The poor boy sandwiches—oysters, beef, ham, cheese, and what not—sell for a dollar. Back then they cost you fifteen cents and made a filling lunch. But it was not the low cost of food that kept me in the Quarter until I married. It was the men and women I met who were the giants in the land. I, a cub, could sit in a smoky living room or kitchen with Roark Bradford, with Lyle Saxon, with Sherwood Anderson and William Faulkner, Bruce Manning and his novelist wife, Gwen Bristow, the poet John McClure, and with William Spratling, and Carl Carmer and Oliver La Farge.

And now go back to the deck of a ferryboat of the 1920s that shuttled across the river between Natchez and Vidalia on the Louisiana shore. Three boys are clustered on the deck and they are keeping a close watch on the deck officer and the deckhands. Neither the officer nor the hands know that underneath flowing shirts and khaki pants the youths are wearing the long-sleeved swimsuits of the time. And if they have noticed the large skiff, bearing two young oarsmen who seem to be loitering close by the ferry's course, they show no concern. One of the boys says "Now!" The three strip off pants and shirts and jump overboard, striking out wildly when they hit the water, so as to evade the stern paddle wheels. The skiff moves toward them, and from the deck of the ferry arise angry yells. The skiff makes rendezvous with the swimmers before the ferry can change its course and one of the rowers calls loudly, "It's okay, we're going with them all the way."

And so the skiff did, making a landing, like a mother duck, with her three swimmers close by. The boys trudge on the white sand, and one of the swimmers says, "Gosh, we've swum the river," and sits down, breathing unevenly. And what he says is true except for the first 200 yards or so before they jumped.

To me this is yesterday. I was one of the three boys. If my own sons ever tried it, I'd whale river sand out of their pants for a whole afternoon and tell them, "I'm doing it because boys can't stand up to the Mississippi like they could in my day." I doubt the truth of such a statement. All I know is that in that summer hour when I was fourteen, life was more adventurous and more romantic than any other time in my life.

And there is romance of another kind—sunken treasure buried in the silt of the Mississippi, relics of maritime disaster and tragedy. A trove of half a million dollars in lead lies beneath the bridge below Greenville, and it has not been too long since a drastic change in an upriver channel revealed scores of hogsheads of century-old whiskey that is better now than it was when it was distilled.

Whole streets and even villages lie beneath the meandering river, and towns like Arkansas City are ghost towns that the river and its shipping have left. Upper River cities like Burlington and Davenport and Quincy and little Galena can still remember their days of steamboat glory.

The changed life of these river towns is nonetheless good, though somehow tomorrow's romance has not yet made fiction of the earthy reality of today. This, too, will build legends of the river and its people.

*At Arkansas City, Arkansas*

# The Towns

Seaward flows the river through a country made rich by its riches, through a nation made one on its shores; the river, water passageway for peoples who opened farms and built cities; the river, highway for old cultures here transformed, becoming different, now, American.

Lake Itasca. Birthplace of the Mississippi. This region is heartland America. The heterogeneous St. Paul, La Crosse, Prairie du Chien, and Dubuque reveal readily the Gallic origins of their names, as do St. Louis and Cape Girardeau far to the south. New Madrid dates from the years of Spanish domination, and Fayville, Illinois, was once called Santa Fe; Minneapolis and Keokuk speak for the displaced Indians, as do Davenport and Fort Madison for the Anglo-American pioneers.

What do these river settlements spell now?

As with the rest on and on downstream, they have the common identity of being Mississippi River towns. Along the shared river the hold-heavy barges load and unload. Here, commerce is ever attuned to the river, but differences exist and persist.

At Minneapolis and St. Paul the Mississippi is rich with the bearers of inland commerce, and across it leaps the first bridge to span the mightiest of streams, which in its upper reaches is more tranquil and clear than mighty and muddy.

Minneapolis, which had the Falls of St. Anthony to power its early industries, and state capital St. Paul, at the head of navigation on the Mississippi, have little in common with the great metropolis of St. Louis to the south or with the lesser upriver communities—neither now nor at the time of their beginning. This was farming land for men who clung to and guided their sod-busters and harrows and discs, which they early began to make for themselves out of iron from Mississippi earth. Blond men from Norway and Sweden and Germany and the Danish peninsula, strong peasant men who loved the breath of liberty and the good feel of earth and who stood determined that here in the northern reaches of America they would build a proud society for their children, a culture that they had not themselves known. Go sometime to the mammoth University of Minnesota and to East-related Carleton College, which is not on the river but nearby within the borders of Minnesota, and see for yourself what these hard-thewed Scandinavians have created that their children's minds may become strong. Go to St. Olaf, the college of the Norwegians, and to Catholic Marquette. Go to the wide-ranging farms, green with the corn of August, golden with the wheat of winter;

*Dubuque, Iowa*

go to a riverfront and discover here from earth and here from water what it is like to love and be nurtured by a newly conquered land.

Even back in 1805, when Zebulon Pike bought from the Indians, for trinkets and 60 gallons of whiskey and $200 in cash, the site that would be Fort Snelling and eventually St. Paul, he foresaw that this place was the logical point of departure for the Northwest. At first the land on the benches at the conjoining of the Minnesota and Mississippi rivers was militarily consequential and necessary for the protection of the fur trade, but it became newly important as James J. Hill built his maze of railroad lines that spread out over the continent from St. Paul.

Today in St. Paul, along Kellogg Boulevard, the buildings rise and offer views across landscaped plazas to the river. Citizens enjoy all the wealth and the leisure that foresight ought to and, in this case, did provide.

Upstream from St. Paul and contiguous with it, the flour mills of Minneapolis dominate the river. The city's tall grain elevators make it the foremost city in the United States in grain

*Winona, Minnesota*

terminal storage, capable of storing more than 90 million bushels of grain. Here is the market for the wheat farmers of the upper Midwest and the center of the flour industry that built up after the first productive enterprise—the saw-mills which clustered around the falls—died as the forests of Minnesota were downed. And here dwell some of the most sports-minded Americans of all.

At Winona, massive, breathtaking limestone bluffs tower hundreds of feet above the Mississippi; one of them, Sugar Loaf, is a landmark

by which the river pilots used to steer. Here in the hardwood country which was finally over-exploited, diversified industries have taken the place of logging and sawmills.

Farther downriver, where the Wisconsin bluffs and the river view are as compelling as any along the Mississippi, La Crosse, formerly a lumber town, is now a principal grain market as well as a manufacturer of shoes and auto parts and agricultural machinery and other components of modern American life.

Dubuque is the oldest town in Iowa, and is now the place where the ships that ply the Upper Mississippi have their winter quarters. It was settled in 1788 by Julien Dubuque and his Indian and French-Canadian retinue. He had been given rights to delve into the nearby lead mines by Kettle Chief at Catfish Creek. From a mining and fur-trading town, Dubuque has grown to be the most important commercial and manufacturing city in the state, processing food and turning out farm equipment and lumber and wood products.

Downstream from Dubuque, below the iron-works and machine shops of Clinton, lie Daven-port and Bettendorf, Iowa, which with Rock Island and Moline and East Moline in Illinois make up what is known as the Quint Cities. In 1836, on a limestone bluff where once was a teeming Indian settlement, Col. George Daven-port founded the city that bears his name. Today it is a thriving center of commerce, with railroad lines and ships bearing the foodstuffs produced here as well as the cement and agricultural implements that are manufactured. It is fitting that such a rail center should be the site of the first railroad bridge across the Mississippi. It was chartered in 1853 and completed three years later.

The bridge led to the east bank of the Mississippi at Rock Island, near where the Rock River enters the Mississippi River. The area is rich in the lore of the old frontier post, Fort Armstrong, around which the city grew, and in the history of Black Hawk. It is here that the United States has its major arsenal on the island

Rock Island, alongside the main channel of the river. A lattice of bridges connects the city, the island, and Davenport and Moline. The latter, located across from Davenport, is where John Deere established a shop about 1847. Here tractors, plows, and other farm machinery are still produced.

Continuing downriver: to the little city of Muscatine in Iowa, where someone discovered in the days before plastics that the mussel shells there made beautiful buttons. The city still proudly remembers the title "Button Capital of the World," although the industry is barely surviving. And there is Burlington, where the gentle Iowa hills that rise from the river bottom to the prairie become the steep-sided bluffs that are familiar elsewhere. Long ago, tribes of Indians got flint for their weapons in the nearby hills. And here, too, the Streckfus family kept alive the tradition of steamboat enjoyment of the river long after the number of boats tied up at the riverfront had lost all other economic significance for the town.

On past Fort Madison, the first military outpost west of the Mississippi and north of St. Louis. Begun only four years before the Anglo-American war, it was a favorite target of Black Hawk in the War of 1812. And going down the Illinois side of the Mississippi, there is the Mormon shrine of Nauvoo, where the issue of polygamy brought about the death of Joseph Smith in 1844 and a civil war between Mormon Americans and bitterly uncompromising orthodox Protestants. On past Keokuk, named for Black Hawk's arch rival, who helped deliver him to the white man. Those Indians, who loved the wilderness which the white man raped and then endowed with a different fertility, would have been frightened by the giant hydroelectric plant near Keokuk which today provides power for cities as large and as distant as St. Louis. In the western bulge of the Mississippi, Quincy has the wealth to maintain in modern style the fine old Victorian homes which are her legacy from an earlier era.

Then to Hannibal, Missouri, which is set apart by two pieces of statuary and a board fence. One sculpture depicts Mark Twain, who is far more than an American humorist or captor of the lives of small boys. Mark Twain, whose heart bled as he laughed, was beyond all question the greatest of American satirists. His statue overlooks the river in the little town where he

*Mark Twain home, Hannibal, Missouri*

was brought up. And the fence each year gets a fresh coat of whitewash by real boys. The other statue stands nearby, a monument to two youngsters who are real enough to immortalize American boyhood. Mark Twain gave them the names of Tom Sawyer and Huckleberry Finn. Their exploits are read even today in places where almost all else that is American is hated.

Farther down the river is Alton, which has not only factories but the recreational advantage of Alton Pool above Lock and Dam No. 26. Below it, also on the eastern bank of the river, lies East St. Louis.

At the river's approach to St. Louis, Eero Saarinen's great burnished catenary arc lifts luminous toward the sun and the stars, and a man can glory in its American symbolism even if he isn't a St. Louisian. The arch is intended to indicate that this is the gateway to the West, the opening up of the western lands made possible by the Lewis and Clark expedition and the incredible Louisiana Purchase.

The partnership of the Frenchman turned Spaniard—a manager of money named Gilbert de St. Maxent—and Pierre Laclède received the fur rights to trade with the Osages and other Indians up the Missouri; and it was Laclède who, with his wife's son Auguste Chouteau and the necessary boats and men, went upriver from New Orleans in 1764 to establish the trading post they named St. Louis. To this settlement soon came other French-speaking colonists who preferred the rule of Spain to that of England, and later the "Bostons," as were called the aggressive English-speaking Americans who had been encouraged to cross the river. From small beginnings erupted the city that once was the capital of the Upper Louisiana Territory, that in 1804 saw the formal transfer of this territory from France to the United States, that served as the communication starting point for the Lewis and Clark expedition, and that listened to the case of Dred Scott.

Thirty miles upstream from the heart of the city, the Illinois River leads to the Great Lakes. The Missouri River offers a natural waterway westward. And 125 miles downstream, the Ohio River gives easy access to the East.

The location Laclède chose for the trading post was an essential factor in the fantastic growth of St. Louis, which has become one of the nation's foremost industrial and cultural metropolises and the largest city on the Mississippi. Being the natural center of commerce for the Midwest, St. Louis was, by the middle of the nineteenth century, the great river port of the Central Plains. The river traffic here, as elsewhere, declined after 1860, but today it is again a monumental factor in the life of the city, with gigantic barges going up and down the Mississippi and through the Illinois and down the Missouri to-

*St. Louis, Missouri*

wards Kansas City. It was the railroads that gained when water traffic declined. They became so important to the city that St. Louis ranks second only to Chicago as the rail center of the United States.

On the west bank below St. Louis a promontory juts far into the river, making the cape an observation point for those who stood upon it and a shelter for those who camped beneath it, long ago. Jean B. Girardot, a French Canadian, opened a trading post here in 1705, and Cape Girardeau has grown as a service and distribution center.

Again descending—this time on the Illinois side of the river at Cairo. At a breathtaking geographic site where the cocoa-brown Mississippi and the blue Ohio meet, "the Egyptians" built Cairo on an island in the alluvial plain, its third side being the now dredged Cache River.

Cairo was a lodestar more than 150 years ago, resembling in its real and fancied attractions the French Louisiana of John Law's Mississippi Bubble of the preceding century. The river proved mightier then than man's efforts, puny though backed by millions of dollars invested mostly by Englishmen; and near panic seized the banks of England when the Mississippi rolled round the company's twenty-one houses and three business establishments—all that the absentee owners had succeeded in building on the island. Wealthy Illinois leaders and southern settlers broke the hegemony of the land company, and embattled and resolute homeowners successfully fought high water so that not since 1858 has the river inundated the town.

To this thin, peninsularlike tip of southern Illinois, whose fertility has given meaning to the appellation "Little Egypt," had moved southern cotton planters, pro-slavery men even when they fought, as did many of them, to save the Union. Little Egypt was a contradiction. One pro-slavery, pro-Union regiment mutinied at Holly Springs, Mississippi, when the Confederates' Van Dorn rode around Grant's army for the surprise attack which delayed the fall of Vicksburg. The mutineers received only dishonorable discharges and came home to heroes' welcomes.

In the two Illinois counties above the rivers' meeting are grown soybeans, corn and wheat, and all the cotton raised in Illinois.

On the way to Memphis is New Madrid, Missouri. To its property owners who were victims of the giant earthquake of 1811–12, Congress shortly after awarded certificates for other land to replace their loss. They thereby became among the first American civilians to be given direct government aid. In 1968 New Madrid received, as have so many other river towns, a federal matching grant of $2,929,000 to develop its St. Jude Industrial Park on the river southwest of town and to make sites available for a multimillion-dollar aluminum plant, a major power plant, and a wire and rod mill. Thus here, as elsewhere throughout the valley and throughout its history, the United States, which has made the river navigable for modern shippers and safe for those who dwell on its banks, goes on developing the country in partnership with her sons.

And so to Memphis. And did you, roistering Davy Crockett, as you drank the hill whiskey and turned Tennessee legislator, did you know that one day you would cross the Mississippi and head out for a place named the Alamo, never to return? Did you know that upon these Chickasaw bluffs would rise a city more midwestern than southern in its resolve and achievement of purpose? Did you foresee that a black man with a beautiful face, named W. C. Handy, would immortalize a woman from St. Louis, and that a boss man named Ed Crump—the most picturesque and honest of American political despots, who began as a crusader against Memphis vice, which once abounded—would become a legend himself?

"Mr. Crump don't 'low no easy riders here
Mr. Crump don't 'low no easy riders here
I don't care what Mr. Crump don't 'low
I'm gonna barrelhouse anyhow
Mr. Crump can go and catch hisself some
    air."

Dictator or no, Mr. Crump didn't go get hisself some air. Instead, he strong-armed Memphis into being the cleanest town on the Mississippi. He helped make it the cotton capital of the nation around a middle south industrial center, rivaling the larger cities of the entire valley, and a convivial trading mecca for the planters of northern Mississippi and eastern Arkansas and western Tennessee.

Davy Crockett, you'd be surprised; but you'd probably find the place too crowded and so head for another Alamo across the river.

Farther downstream, in rich cotton, soybean, and rice country, Helena, Arkansas, has been the state's port city on the Mississippi since long before Mark Twain recorded its charm. Eighty miles up the Arkansas River, new locks have restored that ancient waterway of the delta to modern use.

Here is Greenville. Even if this were not my town and the place I love above all others, I would consider Greenville the most indomitable town I know, a city that has taken all that nature and man could hurl at it and come back to make of itself the most unusual small city along the Mississippi.

Our countryside knew floods even before prehistoric man reared his ceremonial mounds at what is now our northern outskirt. The white men who came raised their levees and drained the backcountry and survived the yellow fever and cholera of the nineteenth century and the malaria which was still endemic into the twentieth. During the Civil War a landing party from a Yankee gunboat, whose commanding officer became angered at sniping from the riverside, came ashore and burned down the original county seat. The feast or famine cotton economy made few landowners and no tenants rich—but Greenville, Mississippi, survived all that came its way and grew the stronger for it.

Here is Vicksburg, which surrendered to Ulysses S. Grant on July 4, 1863. Below the highest point in the magnificent Union cemetery, the river, from which the gunboats pounded a

brave town, moves imposingly toward the sea from its juncture with the tributary Yazoo, and the discerning man can learn how close together and how far apart in the olden days were the people of the Upper and the Lower Mississippi. Most of the shafts and monuments raised by Minnesota and Wisconsin and Iowa and Illinois bear German and Scandinavian and Irish names, those of immigrant people who forsook a Europe where they could find no freedom in the mid-nineteenth century and, not knowing what lay ahead, fought to free men here. As a river town, Vicksburg has the added distinction of being home office for the Mississippi River Commission and district office for the U.S. Army Corps of Engineers. Vicksburg's heroic annals reflect an eon of man's persevering will, and the faint-hearted can be invigorated here.

Natchez looks down from the bluffs, but with no memory of adversity save in the Great Depression, when washtubs and pots and pans caught the rainwater of spring as it trickled through leaky roofs and crumbling plaster. Where southern aristocrats and newer comers from the North and South delight in playing antebellum house in stately, columned mansions, Natchez remembers only what she chooses to remember about the old days, and clings to old ways having to do with certain sad, ancient relationships which deny a world of change.

Natchez has forgotten something which makes her annual Pilgrimage's Confederate pageant and ball a little ludicrous—namely that, alone among the river towns, she remained pampered and unscathed during the Civil War. The gunboats churned along the river below the bluffs, but they did not fire upon Natchez—nor did Natchez fire upon them, if only because those who lived there were more Unionist and Yankee and European than rebellious and southern. And while the less fortunate folk of other river towns jibed at secure Natchez, it is good that this was so, else the great, gracious houses would not be standing today.

Nor is this to say that here was no place for

courageous men. Jim Bowie, whose knife could decapitate a man, lived here once, as did General Quitman, the filibuster, and many of his men, and many a forgotten duelist who fought for his honor or over comely women of varied antecedents and complexions. It is a place, Natchez, not to be overlooked along the river.

Farther downstream rises Baton Rouge. What the Frenchmen paddling upstream saw first was a small red stick; they said it was a *baton rouge*, a stick painted red that marked a tribal boundary. Here was a good place for a fort and trading post, and a fort and trading post it remained under Frenchman and Englishman and Spaniard and Anglo-American. Baton Rouge, neither a flatland nor a bluff settlement, rose sufficiently above the river to insure safety from all but the worst floods. And the little town grew into a city in this century and did so in an incredibly short time—a city where the huge, circular oil storage tanks squat in reassuring compactness on the edge of town, and the flames from burning waste at the nation's largest refinery redden the nighttime sky; a city where a notable state university produces sugar chemists, as well as writers of poetry for the distinguished *Southern Review;* a city whose skyscraper capitol rises as a monument to America's only true dictator, Huey P. Long, and remains as a warning that un-American violence can follow un-American governmental practices; a beautiful city of live oak and mosses and cane thickets; a city of industry and politics and learning, quietly sure of itself and lovable.

And so to New Orleans, whose history as city and port is indistinguishably a part of the river's story. The crescent bend at New Orleans where once an alternately insect-plagued and gently salubrious village nestled, peering watchfully on guard against possible enemies, is lined now with wharves. Two elevators here and two in St. Charles parish immediately above the city transfer the grains of the mid-continent from barge and train to ocean freighters, whose presence gives the New Orleans area the distinction

of being the world's leading grain port. Tremendous tankers follow the deepwater channel north to Baton Rouge or seaward from the tank storage farms and refineries. Ships loading with mixed cargo, moored to the wharves, have their

maws open to the entering cranes. And the port of New Orleans handles more tonnage than any other in the United States save New York alone.

But up and down the length of the Mississippi there is more than the handling of the bounty of a promised land. There is food for the soul; there is beauty for the eyes. And there is renewal of the spirit of man, shared by the people of the towns and cities great and small which share the ever-flowing river.

# The River's Bounty

The Mississippi, from the land of pine and tamarack to the cypress swamps with moss-draped oaks, may yet feed at least the Western world down until that inevitable and presently dreaded day when much of mankind must turn for sustenance to the salt sea. Then man will transmute creatures of the ocean—the plankton and the crustaceans and the fish and the plant life—into edibles which have scant resemblance to the basic stuffs upon which humanity has immemorially fed. This may be man's fate, to return whence he came. But before that time, the young and the old will honor the river for its abundance.

The river fish are being depleted by industrial pollution and, some say, by agricultural pesticides, but fish farming is coming into its own. So the tended man-made lakes all along the Mississippi and the crayfish farms in the lowland mud of the bayou country make their own contribution to man's survival.

The earth's prodigality is itself multiplied by the scientific use of fertilizer and weed controls and a variety of other innovations that increase the yield of foodstuffs and feedstuffs and cotton in the valley. Today the farmer along the Mississippi is safer from natural disaster than he has ever been.

*New Orleans, Louisiana*

*Scott, Mississippi*

This assumption of safety was not always true. The first settlers from French Canada and France and Germany complained of the savage river; and France, the mother country, was displeased more often than not by the Louisiana colony's inadequate shipments from field and forest and stream, whatever the cause. Today the powerful tractors of the industrialized farm and plantation and the huge, mastodonlike cotton pickers lumber above the bluff lands or crouch behind the levee's rising, but I can remember other days before the federal government finally assumed the responsibility of fending off the waters of a torrential giant which is truly national in origins. I can remember the life-saving skiff that was tied the year round to the chinaberry tree in my grandmother's backyard at Vidalia, Louisiana, as well as the drowned cotton of a kinsman's plantation.

Almost gone are the small subsistence farms of forty to a hundred acres which cannot keep pace with mechanization nor give to their owners the kind of living which their forebears had extracted from the land. Gone too, with none to mourn their passing, are the ramshackle dwellings unworthy of the name of house or cottage and which were called tenant cabins in the days when cotton and cane were produced with manual labor. The sharecropper's sons and daughters are in Chicago or Detroit or New York or Los Angeles now. Their departure is no longer mourned, but pray God the day will come when they will find a better place in the American sun. Fewer along the river are the majestic cotton and cane thralldoms that once lay, border to border, from above Natchez to well below New Orleans, proclaiming a tranquil self-assurance that will never again be matched.

Down where the levees end and the river flows wide between almost imperceptible banks, the marshlands spread out on either side, covered for the most part with hurricane-twisted and stunted oak and cypress, trailing gray moss in the southeast wind, and willows green despite the brackish water. Here, on the firmer ground,

Brahma- and Hereford-sired cattle feed on grasses made rich by the river's lappings or, in winter, strip the saw grass for provender in the clumps which would cut a man to death. In high water they pasture on higher ridges, fattening

for their barge trip to the stockyards.

Through the passes too shallow for ships and larger boats, wooden trawlers seek out the bays while the larger steel-hulled boats travel through the major passes toward Mexico for their catch of shrimp, which will be consigned to the freezers and thence to the supermarkets of the nation. And luggers chug upstream loaded with oysters from the Mississippi Sound, where the blending of the Mississippi's fresh water with

the salt of the Gulf gives the marine life of the beds the environment they need.

In this land so visibly of the river's making, where each inundation deposits fresh silt, the muskrat and the nutria provide a living still for the French-speaking trappers who continue in the vocation which was their fathers'.

But a newer wealth—which is also one of the oldest—gives new dimension to the delta lands, for this is oil country: oil far below the surface; oil being raised, in the wells that stud the marshes or by oil rigs anchored to the Gulf ledge's floor; oil being transported, by pipelines crisscrossing the swamps and under the riverbed itself, to storage tanks and refineries. The names of the world's greatest oil companies are bywords in this never-never country to which the river brought its promise untabulated thousands of years ago.

Farther upstream green-yellow sulphur, crumbled from the ground or steamed molten from the depths, imparts its hue to the ships which will carry it to its vital uses.

And in bayous and waterways off the river, in the springtime, massed Japanese hyacinths and their long black tendril roots choke the passage of trawler and barge even as they choke the breath with the beauty of their lavender flowers on a floating island of green.

Some within the halls of Congress and some

*South of New Orleans, Louisiana*

outside them deride what they call wasteful expenditure of federal money to safeguard the land behind the levees. This is foolish, for every dollar expended brings a hundred dollars back into the economy through manufacturing, shipping, and agricultural income which wouldn't have been created were it not for flood protection. Most important of all are the present and future potentials in food production and feed production and cotton production. The time may be closer than we think when America and much of the rest of the Western world will thank God for those progenitors who drained the swamps along the Mississippi and cleared the channels of the tributaries and built around their farms the small

embankments which were the forerunners of the bulwarks that protect so much of the valley against flooding today.

The industrial story of the river is not really a new one, but one that had its beginnings with the arrival of those first primitive men who spread across its rich valley. Their pots and pipes had an almost Grecian quality, as the shards and occasionally intact specimens attest. Much later, from their pirogues and canoes and longboats, the white explorers of the Mississippi could see at work the crudely skilled Indians who followed the mound dwellers. The women cured the deerskin for clothing and dried the venison for jerky. Young boys chipped flint for the warriors' and hunters' arrowheads, and men and women together fashioned small hutments and grew corn and traded their furs for the white man's trinkets and firearms and firewater.

When the white men came to stay and build villages that became cities along the river's banks, they brought their own industries. At New Orleans they created a city of crafts and seamanship, and a craftsman's and seaman's town it has remained. At St. Louis grew the most important industrial city on the river, a center of mammoth fabricators that would have been incomprehensible to Bienville's Frenchmen and the Indians of their time.

The growth, of course, is the Mississippi's doing, and it is changing the economic base of the valley from agricultural to industrial. There is no uniformity of manufacture here except that which the river and the natural wealth in minerals and timber have commanded. Though that is uniformity enough.

How great the productivity of the Upper River cities, Minneapolis and St. Paul and Davenport, from where the flour millers, meat-packers and other food processors send their products to feed a nation, and Rock Island and Moline, where farm and electrical machinery is constructed to help grow ever more lavish crops! In St. Louis, there is iron and steel production and manufacture of transportation equipment, including airplanes and barges, as well as the making of shoes and clothing. And farther downriver at Memphis, inland cotton capital, lumber and all of its peripheral products reign. There are also the ubiquitous chemical plants that punctuate the river banks at all the larger cities.

From above Baton Rouge, from Louisiana's capital to the Gulf, the sugar cane's green and purple, from which man has not retreated in the Deep South, serves as nature's camouflage of what man has wrought. Here lies the land where Etienne de Boré, an enterprising and visionary French planter, became the first Louisianian to granulate commercially the juice of the cane, and from his reasoned accomplishments many a planter along the river would become wealthy beyond all hope.

To see and encompass it all by river is all but impossible today, for much of what the Mississippi has fostered lies high on its bluffs or hidden behind its levees. But for those who quest,

*South of Baton Rouge, Louisiana*

there is the Great River Road, which ultimately will be a parkway along the banks of the river from its source to its delta, with turnouts and view points so that the river itself may be seen and not forgotten. In Minnesota and Iowa and Illinois, and in other stretches of the Upper River, U.S. 61, which has been designated a segment of the Great River Road, runs so close to the river that a man can step from his car and put his hand in the Mississippi's cool waters. Farther south the highway lies farther back from the banks. Already the road continues north, encircling Lake of the Woods and connecting with the Trans-Canada Highway. Someday the great dual parkway envisioned in 1938 by an interstate commission will be an actuality.

Meanwhile the highways which wend southward disclose the abundance which they link.

What do you think, Cajun fisherman and trapper and scion of a long-ago German peasantry, when you consider the subterranean wealth the world would have jibed at your ancestors for

predicting? What do you think, roustabout and catfisherman? Do you believe that all this is so, that you can be in New Orleans in a matter of minutes and loll upon the levee for more hours a week than you, unlike your father, work? Does the petroleum smell sweetly, or is it a stink in your nostrils?

Read the charted coursing, river captain, your barges glinting in the sunlight on what was once a lonely river. Read the roll of the workers, foreman. Read the names which tower on the riverside: Avondale of the great shipyards, Freeport Sulphur, NASA, Kaiser Aluminum, U.S. Rubber, Humble Oil, Godchaux-Henderson Sugar, Mississippi River Grain Elevator, U.S. Steel, and on and on, river mile after river mile.

Upon the surface of the Mississippi, the blasts of the towboats are like the shrill skirling of bagpipes and, in contrapuntal chorus, the echoing signals of the freighters of Japan and the Scandinavian countries wrap themselves together to soar heavenward.

97

# Blow for a Landing

Even before the steamboats the river was busy with flatboats which the frontiersmen of Kentucky and Tennessee made to float their flour and beef and whiskey and hides to New Orleans, where the low, boxlike craft were broken up and sold and their lumber used in the building of houses, many of which still stand. In the early 1800s came the longer, larger keelboats that could travel upriver as well as down. Tying cordelles around the trees on the Mississippi's banks, their muscles straining beneath their wet skin, the crewmen would pull the boats back up north. Or, standing on the gang-planks that ran on either side of the keelboat, they would push long poles into the river's mud and drive the boat forward while they strained forward, until they reached the end. Then they pulled up the poles, walked to the stern, and began the monotony again.

Although in 1796 a group of Pennsylvania Dutchmen tried and failed to steam upstream, another Dutchman took a chance a few years later. Shrewd and adventurous and from New York, Nicholas Roosevelt and his paddle-wheeler *New Orleans* succeeded in making the first voyage down and, more importantly, up the Mississippi. But the trip, brave and portentous though it was, coincided with the worst series of

*Near Helena, Arkansas*

earthquakes that ever rocked the valley.

The challenge by the *New Orleans* had its beginning nearly a decade earlier when three steamboat men became partners. Roosevelt joined a company that was burdened by debt and owned by Robert Fulton and Chancellor Livingston, and they turned their hopes of profit to the river lands lying westward, where conditions were considerably different from those encountered on the easygoing Hudson. Roosevelt planned a study of business opportunities; he also wanted to learn what type of boat could cope with the big rivers. Roosevelt would take a flatboat down the Ohio and the Mississippi to make his survey and at the same time take a honeymoon trip—which he did, in a flatboat whose deck house contained a bedroom, dining room, and pantry, and had a brightly colored awning to shade the soft skin of his bride. The Roosevelts and their pilot, cook, and three-man crew floated down the Ohio and Mississippi in the autumn of 1809 and returned to New York by stagecoach and Atlantic coastal ship, convinced that the big rivers of the West were not too swift or shallow or dangerous to be plied by steamboats.

Trade held promise, too, so the three partners formed the Ohio Steamboat Navigation Company and in October of 1811 launched in Pittsburgh the gray-blue, two-masted sidewheeler *New Orleans*. Again the Roosevelts were aboard for a trip downriver, despite her pregnancy and the opinions in Pittsburgh and Wheeling and Marietta and Cincinnati that claimed they'd never be able to buck the river currents for the return trip. At Louisville the Roosevelts' baby was born, their first, and the father proudly steamed the side-wheeler all the way to Cincinnati and back. And then he steamed the *New Orleans*, with mother and baby on board, over the treacherous falls of the Ohio at Louisville and, while he was at it, over the obstacle of long-held public opinion.

But while at anchor a short distance below the falls, the *New Orleans* became caught up in

*New Madrid Bend, Missouri*

the New Madrid earthquake and, as the force of the cataclysm swept around the steamboat, huge waves and crumbling bluffs threatened its anchorage and the lives of everyone aboard. As soon as the violent series of tremors stopped and the river's torment subsided, the *New Orleans* resumed its maiden voyage. Now beset by strange landmarks and new lakes and channels adrift with uprooted trees and landslide debris, the steamboat did not head into shore at New

*South of Greenville, Mississippi*

Madrid, where the ground had been split by deep and wide fissures extending southeast to northwest, but continued cautiously downriver until the desolated land was left behind. Natchez was untouched and its people shouted welcomes

to the side-wheeler and its passengers. Here Roosevelt accepted the first steamboat cargo on the Mississippi, cotton consigned to New Orleans and delivered to that city on January 12, 1812.

For two years, from New Orleans to Natchez, the transportation of supplies and cotton by the *New Orleans* was an established economic fact and steamboat monopoly. Then in December 1814, Capt. Henry M. Shreve brought a cargo of supplies from Pittsburgh to New Orleans to Andrew Jackson's army, and the *Enterprise*, living up to her name, broke the monopoly.

This was the beginning. Afterward came the epic days of the steamboats *Natchez* and *Robert E. Lee*, of the river pilots who could steer their awkward craft blindfolded through a spring flood, of decks piled high with bales of cotton, of a luxurious passage where the food and the drink and the gambling were not surpassed anywhere in the world, and where men died grievously from the explosions of steam boilers in the panting abuse of racing vessels and from the hull-piercing submerged snags and sawyers of the river. In many an antebellum riverside bank and business office the pictures of these notable riverboats still adorn the walls, and old men who remember with nostalgia the now long-faded days of the steamboat era look at them with a choking in their throats.

In the mid-century, blond Norsemen on the Upper River worked all winter felling trees in the forests of Minnesota. When spring came and the river swelled, many of the same men, in stagged overalls and ironshod boots, rode swirling logs down to the lumber yards at Beef Slough, Stillwater, and Read's Landing, controlling the whole shebang with only well-placed pike poles and peaveys.

There the pine logs would be bound together into enormous rafts that would travel downstream to the sawmills at Burlington, Quincy, and St. Louis. When the river was higher, and safer, the rafts could be as big as 1,500 by 300 feet. Their navigation was a treacherous, risky business and good pilots were justly famous. After 1865, steamboats were used to push downriver these chained-together and cross-hatched wooden floats.

Once, the mourners of the past believed that the railroads had destroyed shipping on the Mississippi. The steamboats are gone, but the traffic on the river is greater today than ever, for the age of the diesel and the articulated tow and modern boat-designing has opened up vistas which Nicholas Roosevelt could never have imagined possible.

On the river twenty-five years after the *New Orleans's* cataclysmic passage a thousand paddle-wheelers steamed up- and downriver, the cotton boats, the lumber boats, the carriers of food and feedstuffs and nonperishable manufactories of all kinds. The river traffic slowed down with the development of the railroad after the Civil War, to slumber for more than half a century; so the river's packet fleet, having before the war a greater tonnage than that of Britain, and then sorely reduced by war's destruction, never came back in the old manner.

What some of us forget is that the river commerce did come back, in a different way. A civil war and the railroads all but killed off the river traffic in the waning years of the nineteenth century. Another conflict, World War I, revived it when an embattled America turned to every means at its disposal for the moving of freight. And in 1917 the federal government created its own barge line to prove that modern river transportation was economically possible.

Today, somewhere on the Mississippi, on the main body or a bayou or the *terre tremblante*, the searcher can find every kind of craft that floats—government workboats, replicas of the old paddle-wheelers, hollowed-out cypress pirogues, converted tramp steamships, fine freighters from Japan and Norway and those that fly the flag of Panama. Skiffs are beached along the shore, one beside the next, for fishermen and hunters; boatels, which are motorized and fully equipped houseboats for vacationers and sports-men, are tied up at marinas; outboard motorboats await the water-skier. Here are luxurious cabin cruisers locking through to more distant waters. Sailboats skim upon the river, as the loveliness of white sail and inland breezes are rediscovered. Canoers, too, test these waters as did the voyageurs of olden times. And towboats move smoothly in the channel—especially towboats, which are the queens of the river and by their barges the carriers of as much freight as the railroads. And more besides. America's trip to the moon was traveled partly by barge, for the only way to move the space-vehicle boosters from Huntsville, Alabama, to Cape Kennedy was by river, down the Tennessee to the Ohio and the Mississippi and thence into the Gulf.

Today well over 200 million tons of grain and petrochemicals and oil and iron and steel and bituminous coal and lignite and sand and gravel and a hundred other bulk commodities are transported up- and downriver from Minneapolis to the Gulf each year. It takes 80,000 officers and crewmen and hundreds of land-based employees to keep the cargoes moving. It all makes for millions of dollars worth of business a year for the barge lines and millions more for the river towns themselves, and, even so, modern river transport is still in its pioneer days.

It is my hunch that if the gloomy phalanxes of those who believe all is lost ever try to exterminate the spiritual heirs of Horatio Alger, Jr., and his rags-to-riches characters, their Armageddon will be fought on the Mississippi and Mr. Alger's legatees will win because they have proved that he was right. Nowhere else in the country have the virtues of hard work, ambition, and vision paid off as they have here in the fantastically expanding towboat industry, most of whose leaders came up, like true Algerians, the hard way. My friend Jesse is a case in point. Jesse came of a packet boat family. Unlike many of his fellow towboat operators and barge builders, Jesse had a high school education. But that high school diploma meant for Jesse pay of

two dollars a day twenty-five years ago. That was the going wage for the many deckhands who were eager to get a job that would pay that much cash and feed a man and sleep him while he was aboard, which was most of the time. Those were the depression thirties, and eighteen-year-old Jesse was a child of his times.

The small, kerosene-fueled packet did not serve any points on the Mississippi itself, puttering instead to the tributaries of the lower Yazoo River—itself a major tributary of the Lower Mississippi. Jesse's customers were for the most part planters, and to them his family's freighter

brought basic supplies and sundries for the plantation commissaries and took on cotton in their stead. The work was hard, and while Jesse made many a friend at the plantation landings, he didn't make any money. In five years he was more than ready to strike out for himself. He turned to the U.S. Army Corps of Engineers, whose responsibility it is to keep the rivers navigable and the land behind the levee safe from flooding. Then, as now, the Engineers paid well by river standards. He earned his pilot's license, which enabled him to handle Engineers' boats and any other craft within an area on the

river of some fifty miles. And all the time he was working, he was saving his nickels and dollars as best he could while keeping a weather eye out for a chance to go on the river for himself. The chance came when Bilbo and Gilder, two friends with backgrounds much the same as his own, joined forces with him. A commercial bank lent the three young rivermen $2,000. They bought a small, wooden-hulled, twin-screw diesel towboat and set themselves up in business. From that day on, Jesse and his two associates have been among Horatio Alger's fairest-haired boys. Today Jesse's towing company can count sixteen barges and nine towboats, all of them capable of pushing payloads from New Orleans to Pittsburgh.

Jesse builds most of his equipment, including towboats, in his own boatyard on the riverbank. And on his payroll afloat and ashore are approximately 120 employees. He is what is known as a contract carrier, which means that his cargoes are those of only a few companies to whom he is obligated to tow their materials—petrochemicals, fertilizer, and petroleum products—wherever they want them taken. Jesse's equipment is worth about $7 million and he continues to expand, as have his onetime partners. At fifty-five he looks like a wiry forty, which also says something for the river. And perhaps more important than the financial success he has made of himself, the two-dollar deckhand has done something else. Several somethings. He is a past president of his city's Chamber of Commerce and a college trustee, past chairman of the board of American Waterways Operators, and longtime member of the Western Rivers panel. And he is as staunch a friend as any dissenter could hope for. This I know.

And it was Jesse who said all that really needs saying now about towboating:

"I'm going to build and buy and run the river, more and more, as long as I live. I want my boys to do the same thing. Everything I read about river transportation and everything I see makes me know that the towboat industry is going to double in the next ten to twenty years. I'll be good for that long anyway."

And now for the *Kathryn E.*

He who is about to take a towboat journey on the river for the first time should try to set out in the gloaming rather than in broad daylight. The supernatural quality of flowing water is accentuated as the day comes to an end. The river turns coppery in the lights of ship and shore, and the river and the land seem to glide past each other in opposite directions. There sound the clangor of bell and horn, and the raucous voices of the shouting deckhands on the bows of the barges ahead of the towboat which propels them. But more than anything else three intrusive noises predominate: the thin shrieking of steel cable across steel lines, the muted thrumming of great diesel engines, and the slap of river water under the descending barges.

The *Kathryn E.* is a white, red-trimmed steel towboat, functionally beautiful, and she was pushing thirty barges filled with midwestern grain downriver from St. Louis If you think thirty grain-laden barges sounds small, consider that each barge is 195 feet long and 35 wide and 9 feet deep and the barge tow moves at a downstream rate of twelve miles an hour, a combined cargo load and speed that would require three 100-car freight trains to equal. Remember too that barges are not pulled as a locomotive pulls its cars but are pushed ahead, five barges across and as many as eight deep, with or against a current that flows from five to ten miles an hour and can become, in places, all but incredibly treacherous. The *Kathryn E.'s* barges protruded wide on each side of her bows and extended 970 feet ahead. This adds up to eight acres of tow. And that is especially tricky in a heavy fog or rough water or a blinding rainstorm or at a hairpin bend.

I would like to believe that captain and officers and deckhands are superior as a group on all tows. This may be true and I hope so; but also I doubt it. The *Kathryn E.'s* crew

107

numbered ten, and there were also two friendly middle-aged women who did the cooking, fifteen hours a day for all of us—one as a substitute the first five days and the second the regular cook who had been on leave. As a neophyte who likes both his safety and his food, I would say that the two most important people on any towboat are the captain and the cook. If they are good, it's a good ship.

Captain Aubrey's story, like Jesse's, is what we like to think of as being typically American. He went to sea at thirteen with a third-grade education, which was all his family could afford. He fished with the snapper fleets and oyster luggers and sailed on saltwater freighters. For the last thirteen years he has been a riverman and a good one. At fifty-one he has his pilot's and master's papers, to say nothing of the eleventh-grade education he parlayed from the third with correspondence courses. He is a giant of a man who looks like a retired heavyweight champion, and he's proud that ten years ago he quit a liquid diet of one to two fifths of whiskey a day because his wife told him they weren't getting anywhere. He has since managed to buy two cars and a house and its furniture; he owns a business, has $100,000 in the bank, and is a special deputy sheriff in his Louisiana town. In the pilot house, taking his turn at the wheel, he is the most relaxed river captain and one of the most humorous ones anywhere.

There is no doubting that Captain Aubrey, like any captain, is the boss man. But the lady cooks would probably win in a popularity contest, which is not hard to understand. The crew works twenty days hard running, often not leaving the towboat in all that time, and the men put in as many as eighty-five hours a week. Then they get ten days off before they start all over again. Under a maritime ruling, they can bring no liquor aboard. Their quarters are modern and they keep them clean. For relaxation there is a TV set in the wardroom, an assortment of magazines, and some books. There are vivid views of the riverbank and the winding river ahead, but these have been seen so often as to lose their charm. There is hard work for crew and engineers and pilot alike, work hard enough to leave them too tired too much of the time to contemplate any recreation save sleep. But it is the galley, and the cook who is its ruler—a ruler who more often than not spoils her subjects—which is the haven. Miss Mary, the relief cook, is a handsome, red-haired woman who likes to cook, knows how to cook, and who, for ten years prior to going on the river, had run a cooperative restaurant in Tennessee. Miss Ruth, a small, unbelievably energetic woman and the regular cook, had for fifteen years run one of the best restaurants in Jackson, Mississippi, and had put three now-married daughters through college.

I believe that a man reveals himself more readily and unself-consciously after the set of sun than at any other time of day. Perhaps it is because he is wearier then, and the night envelops him with a near anonymity, and the darkness encourages him to bare what by day is sometimes all but unbearable.

So the crew and I talked. There is Mississippi-born William, an assistant engineer who began as a deckhand and oiler and now owns his own home and is proud of his wife, who entered and graduated from college after their marriage and is now a schoolteacher. He is probably the happiest man of the lot on the *Kathryn E.* There is Robert, the deckhand who retired as a petty officer after twenty-two years in the navy, and is a happily married man who couldn't keep away from water. There is Joe, a lovable and happy family man, to whom the southern Louisiana Cajun land is paradise and who laughed at Dan Guravich's Canadian accent, unmindful of his own. Today the chief engineer of the *Kathryn E.*, he has held every job from the lowliest on Gulf and river. His manners have a certain Gallic impeccability that startled me when first we met. There is courtly Captain Perry, pilot of the *Kathryn E.*, a thoughtful, visionary man with a talent for maritime inventions.

There is David, a good-looking, rugged twenty-six-year-old, who left behind the bits and pieces of his short marriage and is saving his money to attend a four-year electrical school. And there is little Shorty, the oldest member of the crew, who has followed the river for more than thirty-five years and who says he can do anything required on any towboat. He is listed as a deckhand and engine room assistant, but he spent most of his time on our trip helping out in the galley and cleaning up and substituting, always cheerfully, in any task.

Don is a slim, handsome, hard-working deckhand of nineteen who left an eastern Arkansas river farm near dried-up Arkansas City for college, and who is alternating a year on the river with a year in school.

There is young Paul, twenty-one years old, who wants to become a pilot and make a career as a riverman.

There is Bud, five years on the river, who believes that the towboats offer the man with little education the best life he can find, and with $395 and room and board while afloat, he is probably right. He is a homegrown philosopher. He says that the youngster who quits school is a damn idiot and that he'd better acquire and keep the piece of paper that says he has at least a semblance of education.

There is Marlin, who served four years with an airborne unit, five years in the army, and six with the navy, and worked at the Las Vegas missile site.

They told me a good deal about themselves and their fortunes and misfortunes, but I figure that what they told me is their business and mine, not that any of them had anything to hide.

Ten men and a woman, and each of them a story, along nearly 2,000 navigable miles. They are of the breed of Mike Fink and they bespeak an enduring America. I can think of far worse vocations than to be a Mississippi River towboater.

And what does it take to require a cook's presence in the galley for fifteen hours a day and satisfy a crew of ten—pilot and copilot, engineer and assistant engineer and deckhands—who have spent almost that much time manhandling winch and steel cable and chain and other heavy burdens that go into the putting together and keeping together of a towboat's barges? Two menus, one for breakfast and one for dinner; supper is much the same in quantity and variety as is dinner. Remember that there is always coffee and cake or other snacks for the crew between meals, and that they can have as much as they want of everything in the day's offering. And remember, too, so strenuous is their work that not a man on the *Kathryn E.* carries any surplus poundage on his frame, despite the quantities of food which he eats three times a day. Here are the two menus:

Breakfast—fruit, assorted fruit juices, cereals, milk, coffee, sausage patties, bacon, eggs, pancakes, biscuits, syrup, hominy, jams, jellies, and peanut butter.

Dinner—fried chicken, country steak and gravy, sliced ham, peas, asparagus, string beans, potatoes, rice and gravy, beets, onions, macaroni and cheese, tomato salad, biscuits, cornbread, white bread, and peach cobbler and ice cream and cake.

I am telling the truth when I say that my doctor put me to bed on the most stringent of reducing diets when I got back to Greenville—about fourteen pounds heavier, and when I was already too heavy.

Now the powerful towboats pushing gargantuan acreages of man's toil—barges filled with coal and sulfur and petroleum and grain and gravel, bound for the river ports and—by transshipment at New Orleans—for Latin America and Europe and Asia—ply the river so that a handful of wheat from yonder barge may be feeding a hungry mother and child in New Delhi or Vietnam in six weeks.

Thus the American dream of an intercontinental port on the river serving an interior empire comes true every day.

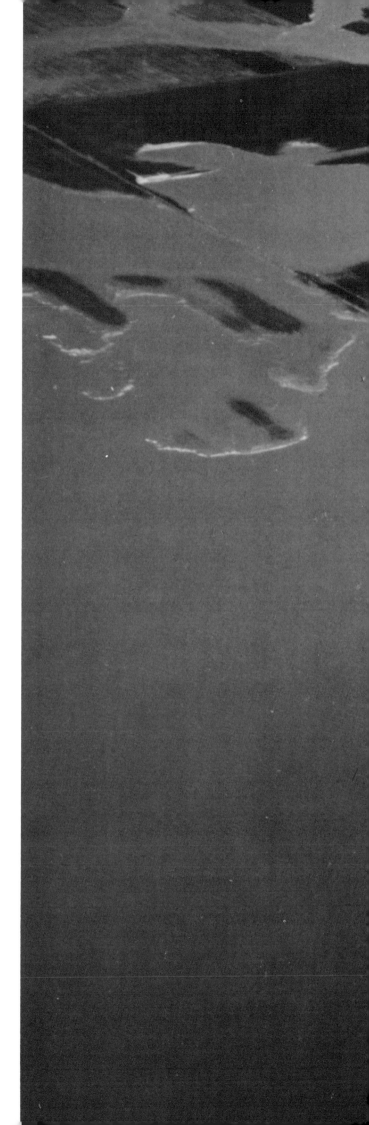

# *M*astering the River

Higher ground selected for early homesites and towns was not high enough when melting snows and springtime rivers conjoined in distant tributaries to swell the Mississippi above the natural barriers its previous rich floodings had precipitated along its banks. Erecting their homes and churches and buildings, the colonists could have placed them high on stilts with boats tied to every doorway, as other races have done. Each year then, they could have watched the blanket of topsoil in suspension roll across the lowlands, revivifying the countryside as of old. Each year the river would have returned in time to a path of its choosing, perhaps leaving landings for commerce far from the river's new channel. But this was not the way of Western man—he was to pit his brain and brawn and courage against the elemental force of water.

The first earth embankments to fend off the flood were insignificant in size but sufficient, usually, for the purpose. Governor Etienne de Périer's levee was but 18 feet wide at its crown and 900 feet long in front of the city of New Orleans; later it was extended 18 miles to the north and south of the little settlement. And all around, filling the swamp back of the city, heightening the levels of Lake Pontchartrain, and farther upstream and down, the river ordered its

own way. Then, along the bayous—offspring of the river's encroachments, where the forcibly transplanted Acadians tilled their arpents—and on the Mississippi's Louisiana shores, low earthworks were built up for the protection of the fields of indigo.

Farther up the river, almost a century later, as man's need for land exceeded the supply of natural bluffs, the Frenchman's response was also that of the later landowners as they furrowed the earth. To the protective artificial embankments, they added more and more wheelbarrowed barriers of soil. Man held against the river, though he lost many a battle. And he is conquering today.

On the southern outskirts of my Mississippi town rise the vestiges of the individual plantation levees, reminders of what life was like along the river 150 years ago when the younger sons of cotton and tobacco planters of the eastern seaboard and of Kentucky and Tennessee, unsuccored and landless victims of a New World primogeniture, struck out for themselves. They followed or blazed the trail of cotton—a minority with money and slaves, the rest with only their hopes and an energy which seems incredible to us today.

The challenge to these sons of the cotton economy was, as it had been for the sugar planters farther down the river, not only in the felling of the great water oaks and ages-old cypress and the shorter-lived willow and cottonwood and in the machete-hacking and burning of the cane. Nor was it only in the digging of ditches to drain the flat fields and in the planting of the crops and the tending of them, to harvest against all the natural hazards of earth and weather and pestiferous insects. For them there was the added hazard of the river itself, for beyond all these trials and testings they also had to protect from the Mississippi's grasp the very lands they had opened and the crops which bore the investment of all they could muster in time and thought and work and money.

They tried to hold their gains with brave

little levees, and the first primitive flood-control efforts were made. In the Yazoo-Mississippi Delta this was done on what was once the old Montgomery plantation, and on others like it.

Mostly on the riverbanks lived another breed, the ones we speak of too scornfully as rednecks and poor whites and river rats, the woods grazers of hogs, the planters of small cotton patches, the distillers of whiskey, the cutters of wood which stoked the steamboats. Along the river they squatted on the battures and, when the later levees were built, they took their chances beyond these first protective fringes of earth, lost all they had if the waters rose, but started again when the waters went down.

And there were small farmers who cleared their own 40 and 80 and even 120 acres, milked their cows, butchered their hogs, shucked their own corn, and lived in self-contained prosperity, except for the act of God they could not of themselves control—the devastating rise of the river which might make them poorer by the obliteration of their property.

Behind such small levees as the Montgomerys raised, and which remain today as decorative reminders of the past, our friends and neighbors have raised houses of a convenience and safety the Montgomerys never knew. The earth for these levees was hand-trundled by slaves to a height of perhaps five feet, and the levees today make a beautiful sight with the cypress that then were children of the forest and now rise hoary and soft green from the tiny bayous which still stand against those stemmed waters. What a Montgomery built, his fellow planters could not afford to ignore—not because of pride, but because the water he kept out of his cotton fields would swirl over his neighbors' lands unless they also kept out the river. Thus plantation levees joined up with and followed other plantation levees in a haphazard, helter-skelter pattern which lasted until not long before the Civil War. Then flood-control levee districts were created to try to make more secure the protective pattern, which too often had failed.

With taxes levied against the cotton which presumably could now be safely produced, the districts built levees from one given point to another and the owners maintained, patrolled, and, in high water, protected them with firearms against those who might cross the river to blow up a stronger dike to save their own weaker one.

While the first plantation levees were the handiwork of Negro slaves, those built by the levee districts were more frequently that of other laborers. Recent white immigrants were expendable. Slaves were not. So potato-famine Irishmen and Chinese coolies in search of work, any work, undertook the Herculean task of building the levees. Hundreds died, to be buried in unmarked graves and forgotten, despite the monument their hands and arms and backs had helped to cast up. For this should be remembered: What there was of salvation in the valley, until fifty years ago came through the miracle of man and the perseverance of man and the courage of man, and not by machinery.

The formation of the levee districts, though a necessary step, was not enough. Threatening year followed threatening year. Levees crumbled before the great overflows. All too often the floods then would sweep away or their waters would cover many recognizable landmarks, wiping out property lines and rights, leaving the owner of a thousand acres of fertile soil with only worthless legal paper to prove ownership of land that could not be identified or that was covered with river sand whereon no crop could grow. The channel, changing as the river tore through necks of land, gave new limits to the states which bordered on it, or sometimes created unbridged islands with established communities isolated from the civil government of the county of which they were still a part.

During the War Between the States, federal troops deliberately butchered the levees, making an ally of the inundating waters; other levees collapsed because of inadequate maintenance. Added to the more direct devastation of conquest, the war-prostrated states in the Lower River's plains had the misery of flood and the added burden of rebuilding the earthworks, so that farms and towns and riverside landings could prosper again.

While the levee districts were being organized and reorganized and levees repaired and conjoined with those above and below, the timber of the Upper Mississippi was felled to build the cities and factories and homes of the continent. Lost then were the all-encompassing pineries of Wisconsin and Iowa with their virgin stands of Norwegian pine whose strong taproots had reached for and held the soaking rains. And in the Ohio River valley and in that of its treacherous tributary, the Tennessee, cleared farmlands, subject to the stripping wash of heavy rains, replaced the forests where Daniel Boone and Davy Crockett had been wont to hunt. Then down would roll floods the like of which earlier man had never confronted or even envisioned.

By 1878 most of the older levees were gone or beyond repair.

Each levee district stood alone, valiant and unavailing—the nation's water was not a nation's business.

The war for control of the Mississippi's floodwaters, which had begun with the raising of earthworks against the river at New Orleans, had in fact become hit-and-usually-miss guerrilla warfare along great stretches of the valley. The river destroyed the ramparts so courageously raised, or topped the sand-filled bags piled high in delaying action. The river from which the whole nation profited wreaked its havoc on those who dwelled beside it.

If anyone perceived that the river war was a national responsibility, there was always the answer that the Constitution made no provision for its waging.

But in 1879 a muffled order was signaled by Congress, an action which, while mustering some help, still promised nothing of direct aid to the embattled high-water fighters. Justification for the partial mobilization was found in the commerce clause of the Constitution which required the government to regulate the commerce, hence the navigation, of the nation. And if navigation—at last Congress said it—then flood control.

But the words were almost buried in the bill which included them and which had as its purpose the creation of the Mississippi River Commission. This commission, headed by a presidentially appointed top-ranking engineer in the U.S. Army Corp of Engineers, was established to coordinate not flood control but navigational improvements. No one mentioned then a frontal assault by the government. If banks sloughed off and levees crumbled and navigation was thereby menaced, then perhaps the government would become involved—but not too much, as the appropriation clearly indicated. The bill, however, did commit the nation, if only indirectly and tentatively, to acceptance of some small responsibility in the river war. And it placed a commission, headed by an army man,

*Near Greenville, Mississippi*

in charge. That much was accomplished in 1879.

For more than half a century the Corps of Engineers had had as a peacetime mission the improvement of navigation. Early, Congress had assigned to it—then the only trained body of engineers in the country—the jettying of ports and the excavation of river channels. On the inland rivers the snags and sawyers that impaled the wooden-hulled steamboats were as destructive of commerce as enemy submarines would be to later shipping. Removal of these menaces to navigation was the Corps's first mission on the Mississippi. Because of its long involvement with the river, the Corps was the logical agency to be given the specific responsibility for controlling the Mississippi's floods.

But not yet.

In the high-water years of 1882, 1897, 1903, 1912, and 1913, thousands upon thousands of acres of rich, irretrievable farmland and many a business in the small towns of the valley were drowned. And the nation, faced with all the many problems of growth, asked only why the lower valley had to swim out of its floods so often.

The onslaught of 1916 brought realization to Congress a year later that America, which was fighting an external enemy, still had not conquered a natural enemy within. Seven years later the Congress enacted the Ransdell-Humphreys bill, by which for the first time money was appropriated directly for flood control. The government matched the levee boards' expenditures one to two.

It was not enough. The enemy was a common enemy, but the defense conducted locally could not be anything but piecemeal. A levee that held in one district—through good planning, hard work, and luck—increased the probability of crevasse farther downriver.

Just as the Mississippi River Commission unified the river's navigation development, a central command post was needed to direct and supervise a continuing campaign along all fronts. The water which safely passes New Madrid is still a threat at Bayou Sara.

In the spring of 1927 the river won the battle and lost the war.

There had been heavy snows that winter throughout the North, snows which thawed almost simultaneously in many of the tributary regions, pouring flooded stream on top of flooded stream into the Mississippi. And during that spring, continuous rains made jelly of the levees as they stood against the greatest volume of water they had ever tried to hold back. Mile after mile of earthworks crumbled and the river raged through the breaks to cover 26,000 square miles. More than 637,000 people were evacuated and 214 lost their lives. Farms were inundated, businesses closed, industries shut down. Below Cairo only one rail line linking the East to the West was in operation. Were such a flood to inundate the same area now, rich with the increment of several generations' and many more people's work, the devastation would be unspeakably greater.

The nation had stood enough. Reaction by Congress was swift. There would be no further partial measures. Control of the floodwaters of the Mississippi was proclaimed a national responsibility, and such control would be effected by implementation of a single master plan. Throughout the valley, church bells summoned worshipers to services of thanksgiving on the Sunday following passage of the Flood Control Act of 1928. Now at last the river people would be able to put their energy into building rather than continually rebuilding.

The act incorporated the Jadwin Plan, named for the chief engineer of the Corps who had drawn up the proposed plan; it placed execution with the Corps and gave supervision to the Mississippi River Commission.

The Jadwin Plan detailed the long-term strategy under which the floodwaters are still being fought. Levees, yes, but broader by far and higher by far than the levee districts had been able to build them.

But not levees alone. Speed the water to the sea. Get it out of the valley as fast as possible.

*South of Greenville, Mississippi*

Cut through the hairpin turns. Do for the river what it has so often done for itself as it tears over a neck of land and leaves an oxbow lake where its former course had been. And hold back the dangerous excess of water by reservoirs, or divert part of it through prepared channels.

It was a bold scheme. It worked, and still works. In 1937 it proved itself when more water went safely to the sea than ever before. Since then most of the engineering envisioned by the Jadwin Plan has been accomplished, and under new legislation the tributary streams are also to be mastered. The valley lives and works in confidence. And because the floodwaters of the Mississippi were accepted as a charge of the nation, the floodwaters in all basins came under federal jurisdiction in 1936.

While the Corps of Engineers has been implementing the Jadwin Plan, the threat of a rising or higher river has been further minimized by the magnificent, protective, recreational and industrial nurturer that is called the TVA—the Tennessee Valley Authority, father of the system of dams and locks and man-made lakes which, as if with an electric wand, transformed the valley of the Tennessee into a paradise for industry and recreation seekers.

While flood control in the Mississippi Valley is directed by the Engineers, the levee districts continue to secure rights-of-way for the construction of levees and to provide close and regular supervision of their maintenance. It is the levee board people who alert the Engineers to any early signs of weakness and report to the Mississippi River Commissioners when, from their floating office, the steamer *Mississippi*, they make their twice-yearly inspection of the whole line of levees. And the levee boards are the river-educated, flood-trained representatives of the doctors, lawyers, merchants, mechanics, and clerks who trust them to keep vigil over the sectors of the river in which they live. The river war must be unremitting if Western man in ever-increasing numbers is to build along the Mississippi prosperity for himself and his country.

119

Here on the Mississippi we must wrestle with our river 365 days a year—to relax may bring quick, engulfing defeat by an adversary which never relaxes.

The river war's paraphernalia ranges from small skiffs to the most powerful river craft afloat anywhere. Some men spend their working lifetime maintaining the channel markers; this today is the work of the U.S. Coast Guard. Others feed articulated steel and concrete mattresses from barges against the more bedeviled sectors of the levee, for stronger levees have made the river angrier. To stop its scouring, the Engineers now place an armor over the threatened levees. These articulated concrete revetments are broad mats of rectangular pieces of concrete bound together by copper wire. They are unrolled from the barges which bear them, blanketing the levee above the waterline and extending underwater far into the current. And before this articulated revetment can be laid, the levees will have been brought to grade and height and contoured to receive the matting. Giant draglines swing from floating perches, and trucks and graders swarm over the top of the dikes, erecting and pressing into place the fortified earthen wall behind which a civilization may thrive. Boats seek out the snags and sawyers that formerly threatened the lives of early steamboats. Dustpan dredges, like giant vacuum cleaners, suck thousands of tons of river mud out of silting channels so the minimum navigational depth can be maintained.

Flood control and navigation: poised in balance. Not to be juggled save by experts. Counterpoised. Lamplight and study: charts and figures and plans. In improving flood control, remember navigation. In improving navigation, consider flood control. Each can be the enemy of the other. A cutoff can increase the velocity so much that a boat and its tow cannot exceed the speed of the current.

There are very definite limits within which the river can be forced to compliance. Beyond these limits danger lies. Opening the flood gates

to draw off a controlled flow through the Atchafalaya floodway will relieve the mounting intensity of pressure against the downstream levees. But any emergency opening of this shorter way to the Gulf could encourage the river to make its own channel, which would leave all the cities below stranded on a brackish tidal estuary rather than on the life-giving freshwater that river man

and his industries require. Today, far to the west of the Mississippi, the people of fertile lands which are dried by sun and wind and the too-infrequent remission of rain cry to Congress from their parched acres for the blessing of that very excess of water that has been a curse to the lower valley. How much or how or where the Mississippi's waters could be safely diverted, without economic danger to the society for which the waters have been controlled, must be studied.

Mound dwellers, Indians, modern man. All have come to the river for sustenance. Only their ways have changed.

In the Nile Valley, the sedimentary deposit of topsoil is directed annually through ditches to

*Lock and Dam No. 3 near Harlis, Minnesota*

sluice liquid fertilization over thirsty fields. In the Mississippi Valley, to the extent that levees keep the water off the land, they are, in their very success, blocking the rejuvenation of the soil. Topsoil stripped from fields in two-fifths of the continent travels in suspension between levees to fall ultimately and uselessly into the Gulf. Someday a way will be found to blanket 270 square miles a year with this natural dispensation of renewal. And as more and more men come to live by the Mississippi, unwitting pollution of its waters could actually destroy the very reasons for their coming.

From the head of navigation at Minneapolis and St. Paul to the end of the jetties at the mouths of the river, the red towers of the Engineers' flag, surmounted on white, fly above buildings and docks and equipment, the heavy barges, and the variegated fleet of the Corps of Engineers.

While flood control for the alluvial valley and for the fertile bottomlands between tall bluffs has removed fear and frequent loss, twenty-eight locks and dams with their corresponding pools of controlled navigational depth have canalized the Upper River from opposite St. Louis to the head of navigation, and have creatively helped to make the water trails known to primitive man in his canoe useful to modern man and his far larger boats. The Upper Mississippi used to dry up in summer's droughts so that steamboat men of old might say of the water, in such a widening of the river as beautiful Lake Pepin, that it was easier to navigate on the rim of a cup than through its dangerous shallows. And deep water now covers such notorious hazards as the Chain of Rocks near St. Louis.

These same dams achieve multipurpose control over the water—by restraining what might cause flood, by impounding what is needed by industry, by creating lakes for a people's recreation, and by directing the flow for the creation of hydroelectric power (as at the greatest of them all, that at Keokuk built in 1913 by private industry). They do not impede the navigation they were built to foster, because the barge lines build their barges of a size to go through the locks which raise or lower them to the river's differing levels. Two of these locks are larger than any in the Panama Canal.

Dating from the 1930s, the United States has developed an unparalleled navigation system of commercial water routes. Today, the Mississippi River system's navigable waters, tying the agricultural Midwest to the industrial East and linking North and South, include the Missouri River from Sioux City to St. Louis, the Upper Mississippi from Minneapolis, the Illinois Waterway from Lake Michigan via Chicago, the Ohio from Freeport above Pittsburgh, the Cumberland from eight miles above Nashville, the Tennessee from Knoxville, and, opened in 1969, the Arkansas from Little Rock, all with nine-foot depth; the Ouachita from Camden, Arkansas, with less than nine; and, finally, the nine-foot-deep Atchafalaya with its own mouths at Morgan City and Berwick. All this, in addition to what rivermen call the main stem, the Mississippi itself, totals 8,539 miles of internal, commercial water routes in the Mississippi River system. These connect like an inverted T at or near New Orleans with the 1,113 miles of the Gulf Intracoastal Waterway, another system along which towboats and barges move from Brownsville, Texas, to St. Marks in Florida's Apalachee Bay.

In the Mississippi's first 513 miles, above Minneapolis, fourteen dams bridle the young stream, but not for navigation. No locks have been constructed there, as the water is too shallow for commercial navigation.

At the other end of the river, the deposits of silt in the delta can block the way to the lush interior.

Early in the Frenchmen's tenure, the bars which silted over at the Mississippi's mouths kept the ships anchored in the dangerous Gulf or inside the river, awaiting higher water in order to cross. The Duke of Orleans offered 10,000 *livres* to whomever could assure the sixteen feet drawn by the ships of that day. And three years later, in 1725, royal pilots were placed at the passes to guide the vessels across, as pilots have done ever since. But often even their special knowledge and skill were insufficient, and commerce languished while bare-poled sailboats waited anxiously.

More than a hundred years later, the Corps of Engineers undertook to keep the passes open by dredging. But the river laughed at the dredges and silted in again as soon as their work was declared completed. Once, for a short time, a different method was tried and the first jetties were constructed at the river's entrance. The work was abandoned too soon.

And then ten years after the War Between the States came Capt. James B. Eads, the engineer who had helped save the river for the Union and who had just spanned it at St. Louis with the first bridge over its Missouri-augmented waters. Eads said he could open one of the river's passes. Open it, and keep it open. He was prepared to gamble. He said he wouldn't ask for remuneration unless, within two years, he had achieved a twenty-foot depth at one of the passes. For this he would receive a million dollars. For each additional two feet of channel depth he would be paid an additional million, up to a total of twenty-eight feet. And he would accomplish this by building jetties—jetties which would hold the river within narrow borders, forcing it to move on, scouring as it went, rather than broadening and settling.

People were skeptical. It had been tried before. But with trade bottled inside the river, any proposition was better than none. Besides, the man had incredible confidence that his plan would work. Congress accepted his proposition.

On July 8, 1879, it was officially announced that Eads's jetties had achieved and were maintaining not twenty feet, not twenty-two, not twenty-eight, but thirty feet of depth. The gamble had paid off, for Eads and for the United States. Ever since then the jetties, extending ever farther into the Gulf and coupled with occasional dredging, have kept the passage to the Gulf open in South and Southwest passes.

Wing dams, made of lashed piling or concrete and jutting at right angles from the shore above Head of the Passes, are a successful contribution to constriction of the mighty flow. Before dams on the Upper River assured the steady navigation depths needed there, just such wing dams were constructed, but the volume of water was too small to effect the desired result. Today those wing dams, covered now by water, extrude toward the channel, making it important for navigators to follow their charts to avoid running into these discarded remnants of earlier methods.

As for the navigator's entry into the Gulf, the deep-draught vessels use the jettied South and Southwest passes below Head of the Passes, while the shallower-draught boats go out through Pass à Loutre. Above Head of the Passes, trawlers and sports fishermen and other small boats make their way through Tiger Pass or other shallow waterways to their fishing grounds.

From New Orleans a new passage has been opened to the Gulf, cutting fifty miles and many bends from the log of seagoing vessels. The Mississippi River-Gulf Outlet, officially opened in 1963, lances from Michoud southeasterly to Lake Borgne and across Chandeleur Sound to the thirty-eight-foot contour of the Gulf of Mexico. It accomplishes for the ships of today what Bayou Manchac at the top of the Isle of Orleans provided for the canoes of yesterday—a second route from river to sea; because of the levees, entrance into the river is gained through the Industrial Canal locks just below the city. However, most of the ships using the passageway tie up to new wharves which provide facilities for expansion of the port.

Modern planning, modern control, and modern navigation aids have made of the ancient Mississippi a modern international artery of commerce.

What of this, La Salle, Henri de Tonty, and Iberville?

*L'envoi:*

# The Everlasting Flowing

From the cool, clear lakes of its beginning, the ten-foot-wide Mississippi first flows northward toward Bemidji over rapids and through water grass and reeds and then streams eastward through lowlands, swamps, and lakes before being joined by the Mesabi Range's rainwater which, as though with an iron hand fashioned from the Mesabi itself, from there commits the river to a southward trending between low walls it has cut through the prairie lands of abundance. Five hundred miles from its source, the river, now at Minneapolis and augmented by many tributaries and swollen in width to nearly a quarter-mile, cascades sixty-five feet over rocks and boulders for three-quarters of a mile, creating the Falls of St. Anthony.

At St. Paul, the Twin City, the Minnesota pours its richness from the west into the Mississippi and, farther down, the St. Croix does the same from the east. Seventy-seven miles south of the falls, a post-Ice Age spewing of sand, boulders, rocks, and pebbles built in the river a glacial barricade behind which the water backed up in a wide and beautiful place which is twenty-five miles long and called Lake Pepin. Chippewa Creek, entering the Mississippi from the east, its current and volume vastly increased as the glaciers melted, tumultuously carried the stones which had been caught up in the ice until, at its mouth, these waters joined those of the river, and its burden fell to the bottom to slow the river which already had slowed the creek.

The winding river has eaten into the limestone and sandstone of the upper river land, gnawing throughout the centuries to widen its passageway sometimes twelve miles, so that at times it curves below spectacular palisades of its own carving, as at Winona, or more frequently turns through bottomlands between 500-foot bluffs which withdraw in more gentle tree- or house-covered slopes from the waterside.

The farmlands of Iowa and Illinois and the aromatic forests of Minnesota and Wisconsin line a river whose waters are not thick with alluvial scourings, but neither are these waters blue, for the blueness of the Mississippi and its history-laden tributaries—the Wisconsin, the Rock, the Illinois—ends almost at its beginnings. Above St. Louis the river advances down the twenty-seven-step stairway of the dammed marvel of the upper Mississippi. Below, the green high bluffs mock the thought of floods. At the confluence with the more ferocious Missouri, which at this point has traveled twice as far as the Mississippi, the burly, muddy Missouri color dominates and changes the character of the Mississippi. As though reluctant to give up their own identities, the two very different streams bicker along together for miles before uniting.

Thirty miles below St. Louis, at Cape Girardeau, the river arrives at what was once its end, for here begins one of the greatest alluvial valleys of the world. Here the floodplain broadens, reaching farther and farther from bluffs to bluffs until—below the juncture with the thousand-mile-long Ohio, which contributes more water than does the Missouri, although less angrily—the now mighty Mississippi, the Father of Waters, flows south in man-humbling progress across a wide land of its own making.

The banks and bordering battures of the river a hundred miles below St. Louis begin having trouble making up their minds. To port the earth is an elevated prairie and a man at his plowing sits his tractor only a few important feet above the river. To starboard a gray limestone cliff rises nearly 400 feet above water level. This geographic indecision continues intermittently to Cairo, in the point of the Illinois arrowhead, where the river long ago decided upon 250 miles of alluvial flatness all the way to the Memphis bluffs and then through another 200 flat miles to the Vicksburg hills.

Now the river presses massively southward, until close by Baton Rouge it begins passage through an expanding industrial complex, a latter-day deposit where oil and gasoline are hoarded in gigantic tank farms. Spreading and seeking in the flatness an escape into multitudes of bayou sanctuaries, but restrained by the barring arms of levees, the river comes at last, some hundred miles below New Orleans—the port city, the city of strange and gay and violent contradictions—to Head of the Passes, whence it makes three major entrances to the Gulf to which it has been traveling for so many hundreds of miles. And eons. For the Mississippi had been bisecting the continent for thousands and thousands of years even before the Europeans' discoveries.

This watershed of the Mississippi River is made up of a million and a quarter square miles, a third of the nation which it drains. In annual cycle across the wide northern face of the United States, the snows of winter pile into drifts on mountains and plains. Rain falls and freezes. Farther south, the earth absorbs much of the water from showers and storms, building a reserve against summer droughts. Spring comes, the ice and snow begin to melt, fresh rains fall. From New York to Montana, from Pennsylvania to Wyoming, from Virginia to Colorado, from North Carolina to New Mexico, and from Louisiana north to Alberta and Saskatchewan, the downfall from thirty-one states and two Canadian provinces must either be stored or find its way to the Gulf of Mexico.

The route by which it travels is the Mississippi River.

Along this long route there can be no complete escape from history. Let us forget the early daring of de Soto, and history is still with us. Let us forget the small nuances that fade from memory, and the Frenchman, the Spaniard, the Englishman, and the Anglo-American competitors for the valley of the Mississippi remain. So does the story of the river which brought them to its banks and sent them out again or kept them beside it.

But attempted here is a portrayal of the Mississippi and a flow of impressions, from the northern beginning to the Gulf ending, that for twenty-four hundred miles and four hundred years concerns man, and man and the Mississippi River.

*L*et us start at the beginning . . .

The Mississippi River leaving Lake Itasca, Minnesota

*At Lake Itasca, Minnesota*

*in a pine-possessed harmonious park at Lake Itasca, where the infant Mississippi begins. From the lake sounds the wailing scream of the loon. In the woods two deer silently change the pattern of light and shade and tree. This is a country of small feeder lakes and streams whose ever-mounting discharge, first to the north and then southward, is no sickly trickle but a gestating giant, an Atlas in the earth's womb. Here the river begins in peace, seemingly, and land and people alike are pacific.*

*In some years the spring wetness after winter's heaviness would spread almost gently up the coulees of the Upper River and through the sloughs and bayous and over ridges marking the old meander channels of the alluvial valley, so that a shimmer of a vast inland sea was all that the human eye could encompass between man and infinity. In the years before the coming of the settlers and civilized cultivators of the Western world, these springtime inundations were not*

*At Lake Itasca, Minnesota*

*Anoka, Minnesota*

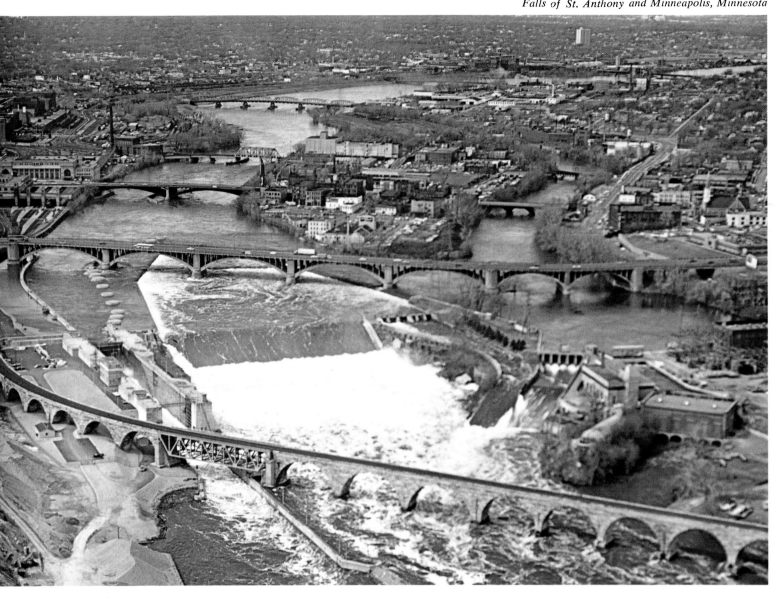

*Falls of St. Anthony and Minneapolis, Minnesota*

*St. Paul, Minnesota*

*h of St. Paul, Minnesota*

known as floods. They were just one more of the
supernatural mysteries which the god of sea or
sky or nature gave to his creatures of a virgin
earth.

Look now at the river land, a region to
pulsate the heart and stir the cupidity of
heavy-bearded French traders and goateed
Spaniards and smooth-shorn Englishmen since
first a New World beckoned to them. It has been
a land of earthy promise for all of its history,
and along the Mississippi explorers and soldiers
and settlers have built villages and towns that
today share a common richness. It is impossible
to live near the river towns and not be stirred by
their unending beckoning.

Yet, however much they differed in
antecedents or tongue or nativity, the openers of
the valley had much in common. They were the
ensnarers of small, furry creatures; they were the
children of the Mississippi current; they were the
fellers of the forest and the sod-breakers of the
rich, primordial land. Above all else, whether
through love or fear or both, they revered a God

133

*South of St. Paul, Minnesota*

of man and this today is the enduring stamp of
our people. What can be said about these
dissimilar yet united folk? Let the answer be that
the river itself is the great common denominator.

At daybreak from the sky the emerging sun
is a fire-red discus cleaving the touchable mist,
and it begins to illuminate a world which could
be the inferno of a Poe or a Dante. In the river
the sun's reflection glows redly, and in its relative

*Near Hastings, Minnesota*

*luence of St. Croix River*

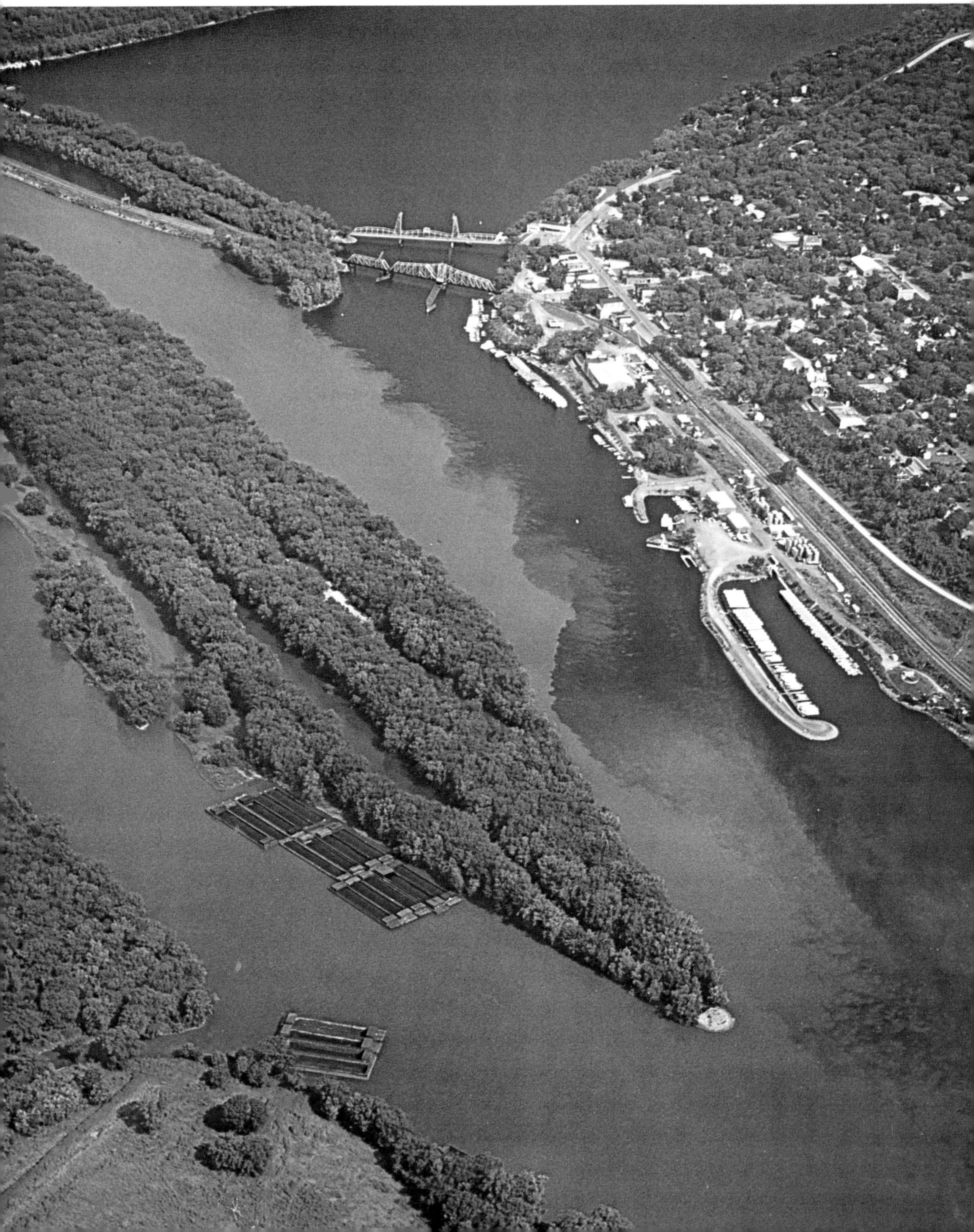

dullness there is a matching quality that joins together heaven and earth and water. Below lies not one riverbed but a meandering, forfeited coursing of other beds which once guided the river to the sea—a twisting and a turning of crescent lakes which were part of older beds

close by the new and where now a man with a rod and reel or a gun can win for himself the fish and the game on which the first men fed.

The way of Western man was not to accede even to a river which had summoned him to its

136

*Wisconsin, near Lake Pepin*

*Near Winona, Minnesota*

banks. Rather it was ordained for him here to attempt to bend that river to his needs, however mighty the contest. And there is a certain delight in the river fight. No man who has ever seen a sand boil erupting inside the levee—with the knowledge that disaster may be presaged—can ever be like ordinary men anywhere else. No man who has seen the rising tiers of sandbags with the river high above the interior land level can ever feel shamed by humanity nor despair of humanity's ultimate triumph.

*Behind the dams of the Upper River, in the quiet lakes which pool, one after the other, to the controlling damming barriers, and below the dams themselves, while the tows go by, lies a water playland of infinite variety which has its own fleet devoted to pleasure. Almost every town has its boats for pleasure seekers, and an occasional showboat entices again the summer theatregoer.*

*The river will feed its own and the friends of its own and many another, for the Mississippi Valley is the world's natural granary, the fertile home of corn raisers and wheat growers and dairymen and meat butchers and fruit farmers and sugar growers and planters of the cotton which can be made as warm as wool and whose seed can provide a fat of the land that is itself essential to life. From the sky and the highways and the river itself can be seen the mammoth forests which we have learned at long last not to destroy. All of this is bounty and some of it is of our own making, and there can be no exaggeration of the valley's life-serving richness.*

140

*Near Prairie du Chien, Wisconsin*

*Near McGregor, Iowa*

Start in Minnesota, close by Lake Itasca
itself, or in Wisconsin, and marvel at the grain
fields and the heavy-uddered herds of young,
blooded milk cows which are the contribution of
the north country. Descend to Iowa and Missouri,
where the soybeans enrich the earth and the
shocked corn fattens the porkers and the docile
beasts of the pastures. Come to the black lands
of Illinois, lush too with grain-stuffs and host to
the squealing pig. Come to the orchards of apples
and pears against the tranquil sky and fields
and forests. Look out upon the riverside
acres of Missouri and Kentucky and Tennessee
and Mississippi and Arkansas cotton, the
soybeans that challenge it, the rice of Arkansas
and the Mississippi-Yazoo Delta and the cattle
north of Louisiana's rich sweetness of cane.
Below Baton Rouge man can cut cane for enough
sugar and syrup for generations to come, and

143

*Confluence of Wisconsin River*

gather in the truck crops and oranges and figs
from orchards below New Orleans.

Vital is the river, known to the Indians as
Father of Waters. Strong is the Mississippi, to be

likened to an army intent on invasion of the
land. But a land-bearer is the Mississippi in a
guise too often forgot: Heavy runs the alluvial
river, pregnant with land seeking to be born,
offspring of the rape of naked field by stormy

*Clinton, Iowa*

*International Harvester, Moline, Illinois*

*sky. Then and now the river traveled a long way, and it is said that every few minutes the rich earth of a midwestern farm is carried from the place of the scouring until down, down, down, the sediment settles on the land fringes of the Gulf. The nature of the river has forever been thus, to carry her burden in her coursing, to drop it in weariness when she slows. In her time she has been the mother of a mid-continent.*

*A man can plow and pick, almost unafraid of flood, down to the riverbanks of Missouri and*

147

*Near Bettendorf, Iowa*

*Kentucky and Tennessee and gaze from the bluffs
upon the dark river, but he must toil in Mississippi
and Arkansas and much of Louisiana behind
protective levees. The Corps of Engineers, like
St. George of old, fights a formidable dragon, not
with futile sword but with mighty machines and
the moneyed underwriting of the richest country
on earth. These are the diverters of the water,
the movers of the earth, the masters or
near-masters of the flood. They speak for man
at his gloriously stubborn best, and the conquest*

*Near Andalusia, Illinois*    *Near Oquawka, Illinois*

*must be twofold: to hold the dragon in check so that its lashings will not endanger those who live beside it, and to bridle and direct it through channels suitable to modern commerce, which also is the work of man.*

*The Mississippi today bears on its broad back more freight tonnage than ever it did when Samuel L. Clemens, riverman, decided Mark Twain, which is a depth-measuring term, was a better writing name for himself. The river cargoes*

*Confluence of Illinois River*

*Confluence of Missouri River*

are not those of Twain's day, when black roustabouts trundled and stacked the Deep South's cotton on its way to the North and to Europe. The crews, too, are different now; but the man on the river has never had it so good, if a man equates a full load with goodness. Nor have the barges been as full nor the towboats as taxed by such insatiable demands for deliverance.

St. Louis, Missouri

*Cairo, Illinois, and confluence of Ohio River*

*Near Osceola, Arkansas*

*Memphis, Tennessee*

The Mississippi River is much more than water and sediment in solution, and alluvial challenge, and a great catchall that speeds the topsoil of much of a continent on its self-destructive yet creative journey to the sea. . . .

The Mississippi is the great bald eagle, our national bird, the fierce predator whose home is on the upper stretches of the huge central flyway.

The Mississippi is a brown winding sheet below the red blossom of sunset in cottonwoods and willows and sycamores. It is a backdrop for the gulls coming in from a day's feasting in the Gulf. It is the swift-rising snipe in the low grass of the mucky freshwater flats. It is the fast-running turkey. It is a flooded primeval

155

*Near Perthshire, Mississippi*

*Near Scott, Mississippi*

marsh where palmetto-covered hummocks are home for alligators and frogs.

The river is a water moccasin slithering in the sunlight. It is an occasional bear and foxes aplenty, and a profusion of smaller wildlife, mink and squirrels and muskrats and game birds and rabbits.

It is fecundity.

The Mississippi is a long-tusked runaway boar whose progenitors found security on the higher ground of islands carved in time of flood. It is the catfish waiting to be taken from the trotline and fried for supper, and the sports fisherman angling for bluegill and crappie. It is the race in a snowmobile over rolling billows of whitened meadow at riverside. It is the smell of bacon and coffee in the hunting camp before dawn and the riding out of horsemen at the opening of the deer season. And it is the small, tender, fawn-red deer which come upon a man

*Near Lamont, Mississippi*

so quietly as to seem tame, until body movement or a crackling branch or the sunlight on a gun barrel gives them shock:

The red deer strikes
from the river clay
Through the swamp and
the brake to the wood,
And the hound's keen
slices the rustling gray:
For the hunter the hunt is
good.

The red deer strains
for the open shore—
The river . . .
Once over the rise . . .
And he leaps at the flash
and the heavy roar:
And leaping, the red deer
dies.

Once the river was the buffalo stamping its purposeful trail to the water's edge.

Once the river was everything but man. Now man has taken over and rules the wilderness of the hunted. For the story of the Mississippi is the story of man, man who needs the waters for fish and drink and a livelihood and a getting from one place to another.

158

*Burlington Mills, Monticello, Arkansas*

*Near Leland, Mississippi*

*North of Greenville, Mississippi*

No one who has never witnessed a Negro riverside baptism can truly understand the ecstasy of primitive faith. Those who have eaten catfish and hush puppies beside a dark river know well the miracle of the loaves and fishes. Those who have seen the wet bodies beneath the clinging snow-white robes, the gleaming gold of teeth in a prayerful mouth, and the shouting of the saved, know a special happiness has too long vanished from our land. This spells sorrow and a harsh divisiveness that does not need to be: So might God look down upon what is so much man's doing.

All around the landmarks of the present are reminders of another day. Once, man-propelled keelboats ascended and descended the river. And laden canoes struggled upstream and danced down with their cargoes of pelts and dried meat. Vicksburg, from whose hills hungry men in worn Confederate gray once looked down upon and defied Porter's gunboats and the blueclads of Grant and Sherman, holding a plump, roasted cat in high esteem while starvation did to them what the Yankee cannon shot and musket and bayonet could not. Natchez. St. Francisville, where by a miracle of grace a cannonball from a gunboat fell upon a church's chancel and did not explode.

Now the monstrous towboats hold sway upon the Mississippi . . . the serpentine, snub-nosed river tows . . . the levees . . . the engulfing wilderness . . . the infrequent towns and villages and the rare small cities . . . the alluvial richness of tilled fields, where the white-gold of cotton built the mansions of days gone by, and where lush purple wisteria still survives . . . the shore lights that come on for an hour and then are extinguished . . . the muskrat at the waterside and the white heron against the green and brown of the forest. This river, the

*Lake Ferguson, Greenville, Mississippi*

160

*enville, Mississippi*

*Ashbrook Island, Mississippi*

*Mississippi, still the greatest of our water highways—without it the valley would not be the promised land of the future.*

*Southward is a new and different land, a land where the rank smell of petroleum lies heavy above the soil, a land of steel and concrete and intricately machined equipment. Nearby and below Baton Rouge sprawl shipyards and the petrochemical plants whose names are legion. They are the purveyors of a different dream, the spellers of the new words that stand for income*

*At Natchez, Mississippi*

*Vicksburg, Mississippi*

*and hope and nostalgia and an old longing. The
words are today and tomorrow and there is
yesterday in them.*

*The sounds of the river exercise an almost
mesmeric function for the talker and listener on
a towboat, punctuating the evening and the
spoken word with the soughing of the river and
the moaning of metal, the rumbling of the
engines, now gentle, now pulsating, and the
intermittent lesser sounds—the voice of captain
or pilot in amiable, unofficial radio conversation
with friends in an approaching tow which will
soon glide past, the guffaw from the wardroom of
a towboat when a scatological jest has not
gone unappreciated. And on the big river on a
companion tow or on a pleasure boat headed for
the Gulf and Florida, a man talks to you about
himself and his thoughts about life. Good food,
good working conditions, good quarters, and, in
between, as good a time in St. Louis and
Memphis and Greenville and Baton Rouge and
New Orleans as any deckhand could hope for,
and what else do you want, Bucko? Not even the
legendary Mike Fink could ask for more, and
this is all the river's doing.*

*The purple sugarcane adorns the river south
from Baton Rouge, and some of the old homes
still stand. A few of the sugar-built homes which
gave way to fire and failure and neglect have
been restored by the wealthy, not as homes for
planters but as beautiful playthings for the new
privileged classes of the river. Among them proud
ghosts move. Across the lawns the wraiths ride to
confer with overseers, to determine next year's
planting, to note the condition of a sick slave,
and always with one eye on the river beyond the*

Natchez Trace, Mississippi

Longwood, Natchez, Mississippi

*International Paper, Natchez, Mississippi*

*Humble Oil, Baton Rouge, Louisiana*

*South of Natchez, Mississippi*

batture and the levees which each planter
compounded around his own land. Here man
proposed and the river, which may be another
way of saying God, disposed.

*The geometrically precise plots of sugar
fields lie in their olden beauty, but between them
the orderliness of the earth has become vastly
changed by industrial hegemony. And on the river*

*Shadows on the Teche, New Iberia, Louisiana*

where once the paddle-wheeler's blast was the only summons to man, today's deep-keeled craft traffic to and from the sea. And along the ancient bayous cut off from the parent Mississippi, the crew boats and cabin cruisers, shrimp boats and the Lafitte skiffs glide through passages the river once knew. And graveyards keep the men who used these ancient waterways.

Because they learned not to be afraid of the river even in its untamed days, men built teeming cities in its valley—Minneapolis and Davenport, Moline, St. Louis, Memphis, and Baton Rouge and, nearer to the mouth, New Orleans. While every man has a right to declare this place more blessed than that one, few today dispute the Creole charm of New Orleans beside a river that is as American as johnnycake and fried catfish.

Downstream, downstream—the eternal amalgam of water and earth, of lakes and bayous

168

*Near La Place, Louisiana*

*Napoleonville, Louisiana*

and swamps and terre tremblante *close by the hungry sea . . . the three mouths of the river . . . the lighthouse faithful to the ceaseless southward flow of water . . . the freighters heading northward with cargoes from the wharves of everywhere, ready to clear their holds to bear the hoard of the American continents.*

*And now at land's end, the brown,*

New Orleans, Louisiana

silt-streaked river begins to meet the sea. The sediment coalesces as fresh and salt water meet, thrusting into the Gulf the long-borne earth of a mid-continent and removing all trace of the immense scourings from the river's valley within a mile. . . . In the offshore Gulf, the oil rigs draw the wealth from the bowels of the continent. In the azure Gulf, the instinctive

*Three Passes, south of Venice, Louisiana*

*South Pass, Louisiana*

*harmony of man and nature and the incredible mind of man . . . and high above, to a downward plunging sky above the river I love in a land I love, I say as if it were a prayer:*

*Blessed are we among all the peoples. . . .*

*In the sky above the river you, a man, become the river god. More, you are all gods in one, for in the brown and everlasting, flowing river is the proof of destiny and it is yours.*

*Mississippi, Mississippi. . . .*

Terre tremblante, *near mouth of Mississippi River*

*Gulf of Mexico*

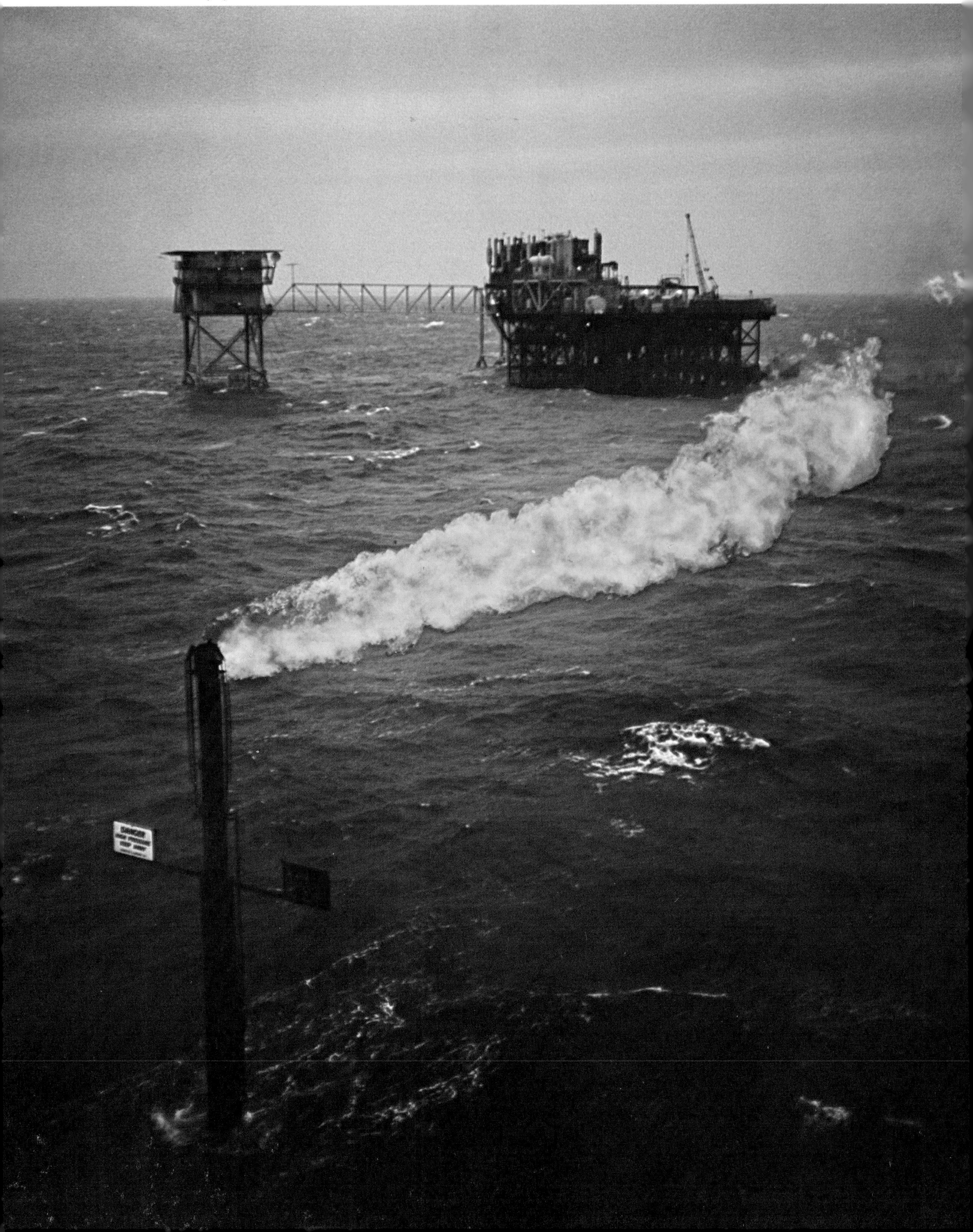